Social Emotional Learning and Servant Leadership

Social Emotional Learning and Servant Leadership

True Stories from the Classroom

Edited by
Rocky Wallace

With
Valerie Flanagan
Robin Magruder

ROWMAN & LITTLEFIELD
Lanham • Boulder • New York • London

Published by Rowman & Littlefield
An imprint of The Rowman & Littlefield Publishing Group, Inc.
4501 Forbes Boulevard, Suite 200, Lanham, Maryland 20706
www.rowman.com

86-90 Paul Street, London EC2A 4NE, United Kingdom

British Library Cataloguing in Publication Information Available

Library of Congress Cataloging-in-Publication Data

Names: Wallace, Rocky, 1956– editor. I Flanagan, Valerie, editor. I Magruder, Robin, editor.
Title: Social emotional learning and servant leadership : true stories from the classroom / edited by Rocky Wallace, with Valerie Flanagan, Robin Magruder.
Description: Lanham, Maryland : Rowman & Littlefield, [2024] I Includes bibliographical references. I Summary: "This book investigates how to prepare future and current teachers to teach social emotional learning by sharing true stories through the lens of teachers, parents, administrators, and students"—Provided by publisher.
Identifiers: LCCN 2023039108 (print) I LCCN 2023039109 (ebook) I ISBN 9781475873634 (cloth) I ISBN 9781475873641 (paperback) I ISBN 9781475873658 (epub) Subjects: LCSH: Affective education. I Teachers—Training of. Classification: LCC LB1072 .S675 2023 (print) I LCC LB1072 (ebook) I DDC 370.15/34—dc23/eng/20230912
LC record available at https://lccn.loc.gov/2023039108
LC ebook record available at https://lccn.loc.gov/2023039109

*This book is dedicated to our P-12 colleagues out in
the field, who sacrifice tirelessly everyday
to provide love and support to all of their students.*

Contents

Foreword

It is our pleasure to write the introductory section of *Social Emotional Learning and Servant Leadership: True Stories from the Classroom*, edited by my friend and colleague, Dr. Rocky Wallace. As with Wallace's prior books, this text is a timely, thoughtful, and practical volume drawn from conditions and issues that currently involve educational leaders and the schools they serve, and the commitment to servant leadership of the contributors to this collection of true stories.

A variety of conditions have come together over the course of several years to create a "perfect storm" of problems and negative conditions for the students of public schools and their teachers and administrators. Even prior to the pandemic of 2020 and its resulting negative impact on student learning and mental health, the socio-emotional development of school-aged children was rising to the forefront as a top educational priority. The mental health and learning issues for school-aged children resulted in a cadre of problematic conditions across age, gender, and ethnicity.

Depression, anxiety, aggression, conduct disorders, and suicidal ideation are but a few of the conditions teachers and leaders are facing in schools with increasing frequency. Chaotic family conditions, limited opportunity to build and refine social relationships, neglect, bullying, substance abuse, and physical and sexual abuse are among those factors that contribute to learning and mental health problems. These external factors are insidious in the developmental process as they leave internal damage that persists over years, perhaps even a lifetime.

Enjoy this interesting and insightful resource, and utilize its lessons in your own classroom and school. What a huge impact you can make!

Dr. Joe Blackbourn, Emeritus Professor, University of Mississippi
Michelle Ruder, MEd, NCC, LPC, Desoto Family Wellness Center

Acknowledgments

This project has been a collaborative effort with teaching colleagues who share a common belief that students of all ages need social emotional support in their schooling endeavors.

Sometimes this support includes intense, proactive intervention.

Thank you to each of the contributing authors for their "real" stories of servanthood and wisdom. Also, thank you to the Campbellsville University School of Education for its unwavering commitment to modeling servant leadership in following the call to grow teachers and school leaders.

Special thanks to Dr. Tom Koerner and his talented staff at Rowman & Littlefield, as they continue to invest in the field of education with timely and helpful resources.

Introduction

Real problems exist in society, and these manifest themselves in the class-room. The effects of depression, anxiety, economic stresses, divorce, poverty, racism, drug abuse, and alcoholism can all be found in the classroom. In addition to teaching students reading, writing, and arithmetic, teachers also need to teach students how to get along, how to solve problems, and how to deal with emotions. These are key aspects of social emotional learning (SEL).

This book is about SEL from different perspectives. The authors begin by investigating how to prepare future and current teachers to teach SEL. The authors then share stories from the perspective of teachers, parents, administrators, and students. These stories provide hope, encouragement, and challenges to the reader.

Part I

New Teachers

Chapter 1

Preparing Future and Current Teachers for Social Emotional Learning

Valerie Flanagan, Lisa Fulks, and Robin Magruder

"In order to prepare the next generation of teachers to be successful with social emotional learning, the current generation of teacher educators and administrators need to be comfortable with SEL."

Ms. Smith was a first year teacher being observed by a supervisor. As she began her instruction, she looked around the room nervously and taught her math lesson. The supervisor noticed that 23 of her 24 third grade students were not paying any attention. A student was jumping from a chair, another student was running in the back of the room, a child was opening and closing the door, a small group of students were gathered writing, and another group of students were looking at books at a table. In addition to the chaos, the supervisor was concerned that she noticed a student by themselves, crying.

After the lesson concluded, the supervisor met with Ms. Smith to debrief and reflect. Ms. Smith stated that she thought the lesson was successful; she did not mention that 23 of her 24 students were not paying any attention to her. When asked, she stated that she did not notice the student crying in the corner.

Upon further discussion, the supervisor asked Ms. Smith if she had created a management plan with social emotional learning (SEL) embedded. She stated that she did not know what SEL was and had a written classroom management plan, but did not understand the importance of executing what was written. Ms. Smith's observation experience is not uncommon. It is important that new teachers have resources for classroom management as well as SEL resources. SEL resources allow teachers to be proactive when setting up their classrooms, rather than reactive.

TRAINING TEACHER EDUCATORS AND SCHOOL ADMINISTRATORS

In order to train new teachers with SEL, the faculty in teacher education programs, school administrators, and other school leaders must be familiar with SEL. Integrating SEL within education mirrors the art of teaching any concept, as the instructor must first explore and master the task before it can be shared with the learner. Teacher educators and leaders should examine their familiarity with the Collaborative for Academic, Social, and Emotional Learning (CASEL) competencies, which include self-awareness, self-management, social awareness, relationship skills, and responsible decision-making (CASEL, 2023). Various tools and strategies are available for exploring these competencies through CASEL and other resources.

Thoroughly exploring SEL competencies is important for fostering and creating a positive culture that supports growth in these areas. This is paramount to the success of SEL for educators and students. For example, creating an appreciation board to highlight staff and students in celebration of their contributions to learning and accomplishments is a great way to provide support. Staff and student members can add encouraging words and comments to the board as well.

Once educator programs or school administrators realize the need for SEL training, facilitators can survey colleagues, staff, or students to determine areas for improvement and begin with tools, such as an emotion wheel, to discuss the foundation of their own understanding of emotions. Providing time for participants to individually reflect upon experiences involving specific emotions can provide important clues into how participants recognize and manage emotions. Allowing small or whole group discussion time to share these discoveries can lead to further understanding and regulating emotions.

Often, colleagues discover ways in which their experiences can heighten their effectiveness in overall communication with each other and their students. Sharing stories relating to emotions and their overall impact can help navigate through difficult situations, whether this involves academic or non-academic challenges within the classroom and beyond.

In addition to the exploration of emotions and learning about resilience, teacher communities can benefit from sharing their concerns with each other. The placement of concern, prayer, or positivity jars within a common area can provide individuals with a way to communicate and release ideas and thoughts. Contributions can be made anonymously, and norms are established when adding to and addressing the comments that are submitted. Particularly during busy seasons of life and work, the addition of the jar can be an important supplement to daily or weekly time, reflecting upon and sharing what impacts us emotionally so we can become better prepared to recognize and regulate emotions (Committee for Children, 2021).

EMBEDDING SEL IN PRESERVICE COURSEWORK

After teacher educators become familiar with SEL strategies, it is their responsibility to teach them to the next generation of teachers. Thus, teacher educators need to look for opportunities to embed SEL into the existing curriculum. For example, a professor that taught future teachers how to teach social studies embedded SEL in discussions of civic responsibility. The professor had students learn about the five SEL competencies put forth by CASEL and connect the competencies to civic responsibility. Next, she had her students review, evaluate, and share specific lessons created by Second Step. They shared an overview of these lessons with the class.

Finally, the students had a class discussion regarding the importance of SEL and how they would like to implement it in their future classrooms. This was the first time that the aspiring teachers in this class were exposed to the SEL curriculum. Even this brief experience helped these trainees understand the importance of SEL and how it can impact their classrooms.

Classroom management is another course where it is easy to embed SEL training. Another professor, an educator of over thirty years working with new teachers as a mentor and supervising teacher, always saw a need for social-emotional resources to help with classroom behavior. She noted that students often have specific triggers that cause inappropriate or challenging behaviors. It is important for new teachers to realize and recognize these triggers. A teacher can be proactive and help prevent some negative behaviors if she is aware of a specific trigger for a student.

Additionally, this professor found that teachers themselves could be a trigger for inappropriate behaviors. Teachers who used a rough tone with students or not respecting students when applying classroom discipline would often become the trigger for inappropriate student behaviors. Discussing this with a teacher after an explosive episode was difficult but necessary. The professor often suggested the Second Step curriculum for these teachers, suggesting that a child's negative social and emotional responses to them could be avoided. This realization was helpful to teachers, as they were not aware of this important aspect of classroom discipline. Preservice teachers would benefit from learning about SEL and how to potentially avoid these difficult situations in their future classrooms.

Another trigger for students can be tied to anxiety about a specific content area. Math was often a trigger. A professor teaching math education emphasized the anxiety that some students experience in math. She encouraged future teachers to be proactive if they found an academic area to be a challenge for their students. She gave them ideas to help students feel better about the specific content area. For example, she encouraged teachers to find one good thing in a student's performance. This would help build self-efficacy on the part of the student and alleviate negative feelings toward mathematics.

K-12 students have unique challenges, and teachers can assist them if they have SEL skills and tools at their disposal. It is the responsibility of teacher educators to equip the next generation of teachers with the SEL resources they need to be successful. In order to do this, teacher educators must be familiar with SEL themselves. The CASEL Framework and Second Step Curriculum are a great place to start.

If Ms. Smith from the opening scenario had been trained with SEL prior to her first year of teaching, she would have had the tools and training to make her observation and first year more successful.

CHAPTER SUMMARY

Proactive social emotional learning strategies make a significant positive difference in the classroom. Thus, educator programs have a responsibility to current and preservice teachers to provide quality professional development in the SEL domain. Additionally, school administrators are responsible for ensuring that their faculty have the training and resources they need to successfully embed SEL in their classrooms.

QUESTIONS FOR REFLECTION

1. What challenges do current and future teachers face that can be solved with SEL?
2. What tools and resources are available for current and future teachers to learn more about SEL?
3. How can teacher educators and administrators prepare the next generation of teachers to be confident in SEL?

REFERENCES

Collaborative for Academic, Social, and Emotional Learning. (2023). *What is the CASEL framework?* https://casel.org/fundamentals-of-sel/what-is-the-casel-framework/

Committee for Children. (2021). *Second Step K–grade 5 resiliency activities.* https://cfccdn.blob.core.windows.net/static/pdf/free-sel-resources/second-step-free-resources-gk-g05-covid-resilience-activities.pdf

Chapter 2

Understanding Teacher Emotional Stress

Chuck Hamilton

"One caring teacher can make a world of difference in the life of a student."

Ron started the day as usual in his new career as a middle school teacher by reviewing his goals for the day. He wanted to inspire his students and get them excited about learning. Since this was his first year teaching, Ron relied tremendously on his preservice experiences and coaching from his collegiate preparation. He realized pretty quickly that in his first year as the lead teacher in his own classroom, there were challenges he was shielded from while training in college.

As bad as it felt to acknowledge, there was a part of Ron hoping a particular student would be absent that first day—actually, almost every day. The student had a way of making teachers feel inadequate and kept the other students on edge with his quirky behavior and "off-the-wall" questions and comments. Ron could already feel his anxiety rising and had not even made it to the school parking lot.

"Greetings, class. Today we will continue our work with geometry—looking at the relationships between regular figures. Before we start, does anyone have a question from previous work for the good of the group?" Ron knew opening the floor to these students could be interesting, but he wanted them to be a part of their own learning and take charge of their role as partners in the class. As expected, Parker, the challenging student, posed the first question, "Mr. Ron, do you always wear brown shoes?" This off-topic question got the giggles from classmates the kid wanted and put his teacher on guard quickly. Ron barked, "Parker, that has nothing to do with the prompt and does not deserve a response from me."

Unfortunately, Ron's frustration was apparent to the class and did not set the tone he wanted for learning and productive mathematical discourse. Ron really wanted to make a difference with students but found Parker to be especially challenging and frustrating. He decided to ask for help, something he hated to do. So he went to the counselor's office.

"Mrs. Porter, can I get some time with you to discuss a student?"

"Absolutely, students are my favorite topic!" So, with a little trepidation, Ron started explaining his issues and concerns about working with Parker. Mrs. Porter listened quietly and showed genuine interest in the dilemma.

"First, what do you know about Parker beyond your classroom?" This question kind of threw Ron off guard, but he answered honestly.

"I don't really know him beyond my time with him here at school, why?"

Mrs. Porter explained how teachers have to consider what challenges students have coming from home. She shared a profound insight for Ron at this point in his young career. "Students have unique challenges in their homes, and they're not strictly based on economic stability or parental education level. Although these may have a place in a child's interpretation of their own value and place in society, sometimes it is our response and reaction to the student that can affect their ability to cope and mature."

Wow, this really challenged Ron's beliefs about teaching and how it was much more expansive than content curriculum and classroom management. This meeting with Mrs. Porter, the school's sage counselor, prompted him to explore his beliefs and how important he was, beyond teaching mathematical skills, to his impressionable students. He vowed to find ways to redirect Parker and others and encourage them to see others with empathy and not as adversaries.

Part of this adjustment meant Ron changing his own behaviors and actions when in and out of the classroom. He started by listening more to student conversations before class, in the hallways, in the cafeteria, and on bus duty. Specifically, he talked to Parker with fewer directives and admonitions but more about his interests, hobbies, and goals.

"Mr. Ron, I like sports and would like to work in construction. Do you like sports?" This was just one of many conversations the two had during the school year.

"Parker, those are interesting to me as well. I play sports like softball, tennis, and golf now, and when I was in high school and college I worked summers on construction sites to earn spending money."

Ron didn't know if being aware of student interests and getting more background on their lives helped make for better mathematicians, but it did create a more positive classroom environment. He realized that his reactions, discussions, and willingness to be more emotionally involved modeled for students a better way of socially interacting and being emotionally invested in their peers and the school community. Classroom participation improved, and students became more appreciative of each other's contributions in cooperative groups. Parker, as a prime example, excelled in the second term in the classroom and became a better leader among his peers.

Ms. Porter and Ron met several times over the rest of the school year and discussed ways he could learn more about his students and what influenced their social interactions and emotional responses. He found that his understanding of human development expanded beyond his college courses and personal experiences. Committing to Parker emotionally and improving social interactions beyond the classroom with him was challenging, but the results were worth the effort. He no longer dreaded seeing the boy in class, which made his whole day better. And he used the same approach with all the students who interacted with him throughout the day.

But the greatest confirmation of Ron's efforts to help Parker grow emotionally and socially occurred several years later. About twenty years passed, and one day Parker was in line behind Ron and his wife at a fast-food restaurant. Ron felt someone poke on his back. He turned around and there stood grown-up Parker with a huge grin on his face.

"Mr. Ron, I thought that was you. I want to introduce you to my wife and kids." Ron could sense the pride the young man had in sharing his family with him.

Parker said, "I want to say how sorry I am for being so annoying in your class. Kids, this is the teacher that helped me grow up."

Then Parker's wife said, "I am glad to meet you. Parker talks about you when we are discussing our kids, and how he wants to be like you for them."

These comments from an off-chance meeting in a fast-food restaurant line validated for Ron the true worth of teachers. In any environment—schools, churches, ballfields, or anywhere impressionable young folks are looking for guidance, even if they don't realize it themselves—adults and peers alike can make the difference in a life, family, and community.

CHAPTER SUMMARY

A new teacher is challenged in his high school math class by a rowdy student and seeks advice from his school counselor. With her help, he quickly understands the variable of building connections with students as well as teaching academics, which will make a huge difference for the remainder of the school year and beyond.

QUESTIONS FOR REFLECTION

1. As an individual, how can you engage students in productive emotional responses?
2. Are teachers provided with the resources to address social and emotional learning?
3. Whom did you look to for your social and emotional support as a teacher or administrator?

FURTHER READING

Craemer, M. (2020). *Emotional intelligence in the workplace*. Rockridge Press.

Chapter 3

Who's Going to Win?

Jeff Wiesman

"Often, the students that give teachers the most difficult time in class
are the ones with the hardest stories."

Ms. Hunter's student teaching experience was indeed a challenging learning
opportunity. She was an education major hoping to become a high school
English teacher, and she learned many lessons about how to effectively lead
a classroom full of teenagers with all sorts of different backgrounds and life
experiences. As part of her sixteen-week student teaching internship, she
was placed with Mr. Baker, a veteran teacher who had taught for over fifteen
years. Mr. Baker was an excellent model and classroom mentor, and it was
about three weeks into Ms. Hunter's placement when she learned one valuable lesson in particular.

During the last class of the day on a Thursday, she was talking about the
characters in Shakespeare's *Hamlet* when she observed one of her eleventh
grade students, Mike, texting on his cell phone. Mike sat in the back corner
of the class, and he was trying to inconspicuously text a friend with his phone
on his lap under the desk. Ms. Hunter initially ignored the misbehavior, but
after the third occurrence, she tried to regain his attention.

She firmly asked, "Mike, can you please put your cell phone in your
backpack?"

Mike immediately replied, "What are you talking about?"

"Mike, I saw you texting."

"I didn't have my cell phone out."

"I want you to do well in class, so please keep your cell phone away."

"I told you, I didn't have my cell phone out. Besides, I don't see the point
in learning this stuff anyway!"

Mike was blatantly lying, so the back-and-forth conversation continued for another minute or two, as neither party wanted to cede power and both felt like they had to have the last word. The cooperating teacher, Mr. Baker, then intervened, and the class continued and finished without further distractions.

After the class was over, Ms. Hunter met with Mr. Baker to debrief the lesson and discuss the events of the period. Mr. Baker started the conversation.

"I had the opportunity to coach Mike in football last year, and during the course of the season, I learned that he has had a difficult life. The dad is absent from the home, and when he does make an appearance, he is often verbally abusive. Mike's mom has to work multiple jobs to support the family, and so he feels like his life is chaotic and out of control."

Ms. Hunter listened intently, and with her newly found understanding of Mike's life, she asked, "So then, what do you think would have been the best way to deal with this situation?"

Mr. Baker responded, "Well, you could have argued with Mike for the next ten minutes but it wouldn't have accomplished anything. As soon as he became confrontational, I think I would have given him a couple of options, both of which would have had positive outcomes in my mind."

"Such as?"

"I would have said to him, 'You can either put the phone in your backpack, or I will keep it on my desk until the class period ends.' He probably would have said that he didn't have his phone out to begin with, but then I would just reiterate that those are the two possibilities for any student in the class. After that, I would make sure I did a better job of actively roaming the classroom so students know I'm on the lookout!"

"Does that usually solve the problem?"

"It seems like it is always a battle to get kids to put their cell phones away, but when the choice is theirs to make, then they feel empowered."

Throughout the rest of her student teaching experience, Ms. Hunter did not have a similar confrontation with Mike. While he still had his moments, she worked hard to proactively address his needs as well as the needs of all the other students in class. She tried to create engaging lessons where students would have a sense of autonomy with their course work and feel confident in their ability to successfully complete assignments. In addition, Ms. Hunter learned to see students not just as people who receive information, but to see each student as a whole person.

This story is not unique to Ms. Hunter. All educators, whether an inexperienced pre-service intern or an experienced teacher, have engaged in a power struggle with a student where neither party benefits. It is easy to only see the struggle and feel the need to assert one's authority and win the battle. During confrontations with students, teachers can miss the underlying issue in the student's life. Mike's life was out of control, and he was seeking some semblance of power, even in this small way. Ms. Hunter learned that there is often a reason behind students' behavior and, therefore, they are the ones who need the most grace, compassion, kindness, patience, and care.

CHAPTER SUMMARY

An inexperienced teacher confronts a student in an attempt to correct inappropriate classroom behavior, and a power struggle ensues. If situations turn quarrelsome because a student has the need to be powerful or in control, the teacher should patiently and caringly find a way to change the course of the conversation.

QUESTIONS FOR REFLECTION

1. Why might students engage in a power struggle with teachers and other authority figures?
2. What is the proper course of action when a conversation begins to digress into a power struggle?
3. In what ways can educators get to know students in an effort to better understand the reasons behind each student's behavior?

FURTHER READING

Glasser, W. (1999). *Choice theory: A new psychology of personal freedom.* Harper Perennial.

Ryan, R. M., & Deci, E. L. (2017). *Self-determination theory: Basic psychological needs in motivation, development, and wellness.* Guilford Press.

Shotsberger, P., & Freytag, C. (Eds.). (2020). *How shall we then care? A Christian educator's guide to caring for self, learners, colleagues, and community.* Wipf and Stock.

Chapter 4

The Other Side of the Tracks

Kerri Adkins

"A broken child will cry out, and the one who hears and understands often calms the young one's troubled soul."

Ms. Colton sat down at her desk to grade some papers. It had been an extremely difficult day, the kind that every teacher can relate to. It was unusually long, the students ignored her requests, and the administration was pushing for better test scores. It seemed like she could spend hours at school and still never complete all of the necessary tasks. She let out a long sigh as she looked over student work and entered their grades into the computer. As the tired teacher filled in the zeros, her eyes were drawn to one student's name. "Joey Peters," she said, as if to ask if he was present.

This was Ms. Colton's first year of teaching high school English. She had searched and searched for a job close to her own home but had been unable to find one. So, like many inexperienced teachers, she had to take a position in a nearby county. The transition had been anything but easy. She was given the lower-level classes that other teachers avoided. These classes contained many students with IEPS, students who barely spoke English, and lots and lots of behavior problems. Her heart went out to these kids, because most of them did not want to be there. They were more interested in social ventures than learning.

School had been in session for a whole month, and Ms. Cotton had yet to meet Joey. Several of the other students had told her things about him. He seemed popular among the misfit kids and was known for being impulsive and getting into trouble. Honestly, she hoped he just stayed home. She already had her hands full with several of the students in that class. Many students seemed to care very little about learning and more about partying on the weekends.

So far, the other students had explained that Joey did not have a good home life. His mom had left when he was little. Since then, he had lived with his brother and his dad. His dad worked long hours, leaving the boys to often fend for themselves. When he was home, he was extremely hard on both the boys. He expected them to work like men when they were not in school and had little appreciation for a good education.

As she learned more about Joey, Ms. Cotton found out that he had not been attending school because he was having a hard time dealing with the death of a close friend that had happened over the summer. Joey had been with him the night of the accident. They had been partying at one house and decided to head over to another friend's house. Joey got in the car with his girlfriend, and his friend insisted on driving himself. As they drove down the small two-lane road at high speeds, playing leapfrog, Joey's friend lost control of the car, and it ended up flipping in a corn field.

The first time that Ms. Colton heard the story, she felt sick to her stomach. Her heart broke for Joey. She had boys about his age and could not even fathom how this kind of tragedy would affect them. Immediately, she just wanted to hug him and tell him that everything would be alright. She knew his dad was probably not helping him work through the grief. Not that he was a horrible father, but typical of how generational curses can be. No wonder Joey had been skipping school.

At the beginning of week five, one of the students told Ms. Colton that Joey would be in class the following Monday, and he was not happy about it. She wondered all week long how it would go. She wondered how the class dynamic would change and if the kids would get along. Many of the other students seemed to be on edge when they found out Joey was returning. He definitely had a rough reputation.

Despite Ms. Colton hoping to slow down time, Monday rolled around any-way. Then, third period came. She knew the moment Joey walked in because he was the only student she did not recognize. She could see why many of the other students were intimidated by him. He stood around six feet tall and was built like a large man. He would have made a great linebacker for the football team, but evidently he could not stay out of trouble long enough to be allowed to play. His attitude matched his size. He walked into the classroom for the first time, like he owned the place, and was ready to fight. He walked straight up to Ms. Colton's desk with an entourage of classmates following.

Joey introduced himself as the one that most teachers dreaded having in class and indicated that Ms. Colton would be no different. After she told him that it was nice to finally meet him, she showed him where he would be sitting. He smarted off something and then headed to his seat. He plopped himself down, put his hands behind his head and his feet on the desk, and proceeded to lean back in his chair. This was exactly what Ms. Colton had been dreading. She could not allow it to begin this way. He was definitely testing her.

"Joey, you need to put all four legs of that chair on the ground please," Ms. Colton said in a firm voice despite the fact, that she was shaking.

"Why do I need to do that?" he asked.

"I am afraid that you will fall and be injured."

He smirked, and several of the students giggled.

"Why don't you come and make me?"

Ms. Colton hated confrontation, but she knew that she had to deal with this kind of defiance immediately. If she did not, it would continue to get worse. This was a game of power and will.

"If you do not put that chair down on all fours, I will have to write you up for in-school suspension. I would hate to do that on your first day back."

After several moments of staring at one another, Joey slowly lowered the chair to the ground. Ms. Colton breathed a quiet sigh of relief. She knew that this was only the beginning, though. They made it through the rest of class that day with no major problems. As she went home that night, she laid in bed awake, preparing for future scenarios. She remembered some advice that a previous mentor teacher had given her: "The ones that act like they need you the least actually need you the most." But how could she get through? Joey seemed to have such a tough exterior. She was not sure how, but she had to try.

The next few weeks were not any easier. Despite Ms. Colton trying to build a relationship with Joey, he seemed to dislike women. She assumed that this was probably due to his mother abandoning the family when he was young. She had tried calling the father when he caused problems, but that was futile too. His father did not seem to respect women either.

Joey did not play football any longer, so she could not reach out to coaches. After asking around, Ms. Colton found a male teacher that he did have a great respect for, so she began to use this to her advantage. She even called the other teacher down to her classroom once or twice when she could not deescalate the situation. Somehow, the class survived the semester, and learning seemed to have occurred. However, Ms. Colton felt somewhat defeated that she had been unable to reach the boy.

The next school year, Ms. Colton would see Joey sometimes in the hallway, and she would make it a point to talk to him. She asked him about his summer and how his classes were going. He always answered her questions, but there was still something deeper missing. One day, when she stopped him in the hall, he told her that he was excited about a job opportunity. She could tell he was really proud, and she complimented him. It was still not what she was looking for as confirmation, but it felt good that he wanted her praise and approval.

On the last day of the year, students were moving furniture into the hall-ways so the janitors could shine the floors over the summer break. One of the boys was horsing around, and Ms. Colton got onto him. The boy smarted off something, and out of nowhere, she saw Joey step in. He said, "That is Ms. Colton. You leave her alone. She is one of the good ones." Ms. Colton smiled. That was the confirmation that she had needed all that time. Steady persistence had paid off.

John C. Maxwell said it best: "Students don't care how much you know until they know how much you care."

CHAPTER SUMMARY

A high school teacher struggles with how to deal with a troublesome student, but eventually realizes her steadiness in the classroom and setting boundaries helped him stay the course, even though faced with a challenging home life.

QUESTIONS FOR REFLECTION

1. How do you learn about the backgrounds of the students in your class?
2. What "triggers" often set a student off who has a history of poor behavior at school?
3. Does your school require or encourage teachers to make home visits before the new school year begins?

FURTHER READING

Hylen, M. G. (2022). *The 5 habits of the emotion coach.* Rowman & Littlefield.

Part II

In the Classroom

Chapter 5

Social Emotional Health is Contagious

Kathryn E. H. Smith

"The beginning of the school year can create stressed out teachers, which can cause students to also feel stressed and anxious—because social emotional health is contagious."

Educators have the privilege of experiencing their students' academic accomplishments and personal victories. However, many students encounter social-emotional needs, which often challenge teachers to reach beyond their pedagogical knowledge to carefully utilize social emotional learning (SEL) (Gosner, 2020). Unfortunately, teachers themselves experience workplace stress, which may impact their ability to support students' social-emotional needs (Collie et al., 2012). Schonert-Reichl (2017) explained that teachers are the main facilitators of SEL programs within classrooms, and it is imperative for educators to understand that their own "social-emotional competence and well-being influences their students" (p. 137).

Given the importance of teacher self-awareness and emotional competency, what happens if the teacher struggles with their own emotions as a result of workplace stress? This chapter details an educator who struggled with his own social emotions, self-awareness, and emotional competency due to job stress. In turn, he was unaware of how to support his students' social-emotional needs, resulting in one particular student experiencing anxiety and stomachaches.

The new school year began, and like many students, Lilly Hodge was excited to see her friends from the previous academic year. But mostly, Lilly was excited to meet her new teacher, Mr. Gordon. Lilly had seen Mr. Gordon in the hallway several times last year, and he always smiled and said, "Hello." So, Lilly thought fifth grade would be terrific—just like fourth grade. In the hallway, Lilly passed her previous fourth-grade classroom to see Mrs. Pretty waving and smiling. Soon, this honor roll student felt a wave of sadness as she realized she would not be with her favorite teacher again this school year.

Just then, Lilly arrived at Mr. Gordon's classroom, who seemed stressed as he rushed around the crowded room trying to settle the loud pupils. Every seat was filled with bright-eyed students. After the bell rang, he hushed everyone and reviewed the new class rules: "No talking when I am talking, no shouting out, stay in your seats, use kind words, and keep your hands to yourself." Lilly noticed that Mr. Gordon's tone was firm, and he no longer smiled. Inside, she missed Mrs. Pretty and began feeling very nervous and anxious about her new teacher.

Next, Mr. Gordon handed out worksheets and wrote quickly on the board. He explained with a stern voice, "We are moving through this worksheet real fast today because it is just a review."

Lilly's anxiety flared up, and she started to feel sick to her stomach. She thought to herself, "Mr. Gordon is nothing like Mrs. Pretty." Unfortunately, Lilly's stomachache prevented her from focusing on the lesson, so she looked around the room.

Mr. Gordon loudly urged her in front of the class, "Please pay attention and get on task." At once, she felt very embarrassed and thought she might throw up. When she got home from school, she told her mom that she felt sick and nauseated.

The next few days of school, Lilly sat anxiously as Mr. Gordon continued to establish his rules and expectations with his new fifth grade students. He showed the students his bell and explained, "When I ring it, you all should immediately stop talking and pay attention."

Unfortunately, Mr. Gordon's classroom management revealed that he mostly used negative consequences for classroom behavior. The only positive incentive for good behavior was a movie on Friday. The movie was permitted if the entire class had enough behavior points. Although Mr. Gordon gave behavior points, he did so only on his computer app, and he did not praise students for following class rules. Therefore, Lilly and her classmates were kept guessing and often surprised if their behavior was rewarded at all.

One afternoon, a few peers disrupted the class by calling out. Mr. Gordon became very frustrated and rang his bell repeatedly. After six years of teaching fifth grade, he had not taught a class this large and felt overwhelmed by multiple disruptions. Thus, he punished the entire class for a few students' misbehavior by canceling the movie on Friday. This made Lilly feel anxious and disappointed because her good behavior was not rewarded, and she had been trying so hard to please her new teacher.

In addition, Lilly noticed that when students were off task, Mr. Gordon called them by name in front of everyone. Sometimes, he lost control of his own emotions and spoke unkindly to his students or raised his voice. Given Lilly's new loud, stressful, and emotionally unstable classroom environment, she continued to experience anxiety and nausea. And she feared that Mr. Gordon would call on her again, embarrass her, or worse, take her behavior points away so she would get in trouble with her mom.

The fourth day of school, Lilly protested to her mom that she was sick with a stomachache. So, she stayed home to rest and recover. However, at home, Lilly did not seem sick at all. In fact, she acted completely normal and healthy; she just did not want to go to school.

The next day, Lilly cried to her mother, saying that she was sick and needed to stay home again. Immediately, Mrs. Hodge knew that something else was going on and that Lilly did not have a stomach virus. During lunch time, Mrs. Hodge called Mr. Gordon and asked how Lilly was doing in class. He was very irritated and explained that Lilly could not focus, worked slowly, and was easily distracted. Mrs. Hodge explained that Mrs. Pretty never mentioned this behavior before and that Lilly was an honor roll student, so she could focus just fine. Further, she pointed out that Lilly had had stomachaches for five days and suggested maybe she was having anxiety in the classroom.

Unfortunately, Mr. Gordon dismissed Mrs. Hodge's concerns regarding Lilly's anxiety and stress in his classroom. He was much too busy with his overcrowded and rambunctious class to discuss this matter further. After one week of having Lilly in class, Mr. Gordon recommended that Lilly be evaluated for ADHD. Therefore, he did not recognize how his own stress negatively affected Lilly's social-emotional health.

Research suggests that teaching is one of the most stressful professions (Al-Fudail & Mellar, 2008; De Nobile & McCormich, 2005), and that teachers are at risk of poor social emotional well-being (Shonert-Reichl, 2017). This brief excerpt demonstrates that teachers may experience stress, which could result in increased burn out (McCarty et al., 2009), a reduction in job satisfaction (Klassen & Chiu, 2010), and job commitment (Klassen & Chiu, 2011).

Even more, Jennings and Greenberg's (2009) research found that teachers' social emotional competence is important in four areas: healthy teacher-student relationships, effective classroom management, a healthy classroom environment, and effective SEL implementation. While Mr. Gordon wanted to support his students academically he was unaware of how his own social emotions were impacting his students, especially Lilly. More so, he did not understand the positive impact that SEL could have had on his pupils.

Mahoney et al. (2018) explained that SEL programs have demonstrated to have long-term impact on academic growth. Mr. Gordon was eager to teach the academic content; however, he was not properly trained to use SEL. Therefore, this may have diminished the academic gains the students were making as they were learning in an emotionally unhealthy environment.

So what happened with the situation involving Lilly and her mom? Lilly's pediatrician dismissed any signs of ADHD and provided her with social-emotional strategies to manage with her anxiety and stress levels at school. Further, the pediatrician provided Mrs. Hodge with anxiety support and incentives for Lilly's positive school behavior. Miller (2023) explained that when children get headaches or stomachaches regularly, it could be a sign of anxiety, which seemed to be the cause of Lilly's symptoms.

Comparatively, when students experience warm teacher-child relationships, it supports deep learning and positive social and emotional development among peers in the classroom (Schonert-Reichl, 2017). Therefore, if Mr. Gordon had recognized that he was affecting his students negatively, he may have been able to manage his own stress and better provide warm teacher-student relationships as methods to support learning and positive social emotions among his students.

The reality is that teachers experience immense stress throughout the course of their tenure (De Nobile & McCormich, 2005). However, researchers have examined interventions to mitigate teachers' workplace stress and improve their social emotional competence because stressed out teachers tend to have stressed out students (Schonert-Reichly, 2017).

Further, providing teachers with stress management and adequate supports may increase teacher self-efficacy, which may influence the fidelity needed for teachers to implement their SEL programs accurately (Schonert-Reichl, 2017). Therefore, it is paramount to address teachers' social-emotional needs, as this could be the key to creating healthy social-emotional students.

CHAPTER SUMMARY

A young student is traumatized by the daily stress exhibited by her fifth grade teacher. She receives professional assistance for her anxiety—a condition in far too many classrooms that can be prevented when teachers themselves better cope with the stress of their work.

QUESTIONS FOR REFLECTION

1. If you are a practitioner, how do you deal with your own social-emotional stress and not project it on to your students?
2. Are you trained in SEL and do you regularly implement these frameworks in your classroom?
3. What areas of SEL could you improve to better support your students?

REFERENCES

Al-Fudail, M., & Mellar, H. (2008). Investigating teacher stress when using technology. *Computers & Education, 51*, 1103–1110. doi:10.1016/j.compedu.2007.11.004

Collie, R. J., Shapka, J. D., & Perry, N. E. (2012). School climate and social–emotional learning. *Journal of Educational Psychology, 104*(4), 1189–1204. doi: 10.1037/a0029356

De Nobile, J., & McCormick, J. (2005). Job satisfaction and occupational stress in Catholic primary schools. Paper presented at the annual conference of the Australian Association for Research in Education, Sydney, Australia.

Gosner, S. (2020). Good teaching is not just about the right practices. *Edutopia.* https://www.edutopia.org/article/good-teaching-not-just-about-right-practices/

Jennings, P. A., & Greenberg, M. T. (2009). The prosocial classroom: Teacher social and emotional competence in relation to student and classroom outcomes. *Review of Educational Research, 79*, 491–525. doi:10.3102/0034654308325693

Klassen, R. M., & Chiu, M. M. (2010). Effects on teachers' self-efficacy and job satisfaction: Teacher gender, years of experience, and job stress. *Journal of Educational Psychology, 102*, 741–756. doi:10.1037/a0019237

Klassen, R. M., & Chiu, M. M. (2011). The occupational commitment and intention to quit of practicing and preservice teachers: Influence of self-efficacy, job stress, and teaching context. *Contemporary Educational Psychology, 36*, 114–129. doi:10.1016/j.cedpsych.2011.01.002

Mahoney, J. L., Durklan, J. A., & Weissberg, R. P. (2018). An update on social and emotional learning outcome research. *Kappan.* https://kappanonline.org/social-emotional-learning-outcome-research-mahoney-durlak-weissberg/

McCarthy, C. J., Lambert, R. C., O'Donnell, M., & Melendres, L. T. (2009). The relation of elementary teachers' experience, stress, and coping resources to burnout symptoms. *Elementary School Journal, 109*, 282–300. doi:10.1086/592308

Miller, C. (2023). Anxious stomach aches and headaches. *Child Mind Institute.* https://childmind.org/article/anxious-stomach-aches-and-headaches/

Schonert-Reichl, K. A. (2017). Social and emotional learning and teachers. *The Future of Children, 27*(1), 137–155. http://www.jstor.org/stable/44219025

Chapter 6

Two "Rounders" for Sure

Rocky Wallace

"Sometimes, if a student knows that even one teacher cares about them more than just their school work, it can make a difference."

Jenny and Billie—Dave still remembers their names and can see their faces thirty-five years after having them in his seventh grade girls' health and PE class. Simply put, they were what the old timers call "rounders." In other words, they were rebels, and they enjoyed it.

The two girls ran together, and when in class would do almost anything for attention. Rarely did a day go by that one of them was not sent to the office, or reprimanded.

"Mr. Johnson, may I go to the bathroom?"

"Mr. Johnson, I think I'm going to throw up."

"I left my work at home again."

"Mom works at night, so I'm on my own a lot."

"I was at a cool party over the weekend."

"I wasn't here last week because the assistant principal suspended me again."

"I might be going to another school soon. We can't pay the rent."

Dave was at a loss. In a class of twenty-four girls, Jenny and Billie were the only two who seemed to not even try. They demanded the vast majority of his extra attention. All he knew was to do his best to let them know he cared.

One week, Jenny was absent for several days. Dave found out she was in the hospital. He decided to make a visit. When he walked into her room, her eyes widened. "Mr. Johnson. What are you doing here?" Her long red hair was a mess, and she looked so tired.

"Well, Billie told me I'd find you here. Class sure has been boring this week."

Jenny chuckled. "Appendicitis. Wouldn't you know it! . . . I cause pain all the time, and now I'm having it thrown back at me."

Dave laughed. "Yep. Maybe this is good for you. . . . Hey, when are you going to get to go home?"

"Tomorrow morning. Mom was supposed to be here earlier today to pick me up, but she couldn't make it. So, they told me it'd be in the morning now."

"Your Mom is working today?"

"I didn't think so. But they call her in for extra shifts sometimes."

"Your Dad?"

"Missing in action, Mr. Johnson. Haven't seen him in six months."

"Well, the girls in class said to tell you 'hello.' I'll tell them you're recovering well, and will be back soon."

"Thanks Mr. Johnson. I appreciate you stopping by. I didn't expect you to visit me here in the hospital. I guess I'm gonna have to try to not give you such a hard time in class." Jenny smiled, and Dave did too, as he waved to her on the way out the door.

Dave Johnson did not know what happened to Jenny and her "partner in crime," Billie, after the end of that school year. He assumed they had both eventually traveled down a bad road, and maybe not even graduated from high school.

Several years later, Dave was ordering a meal at a fast-food restaurant, and to his surprise, the girl waiting on him was Billie. "Mr. Johnson, hello!"

"Billie? I thought that was you. How are you doing?" The small statured woman with her short blond hair still looked half her age.

"Doin' OK. . . . Hey, I wanted to apologize for how much trouble I caused you when I was in your class back in junior high."

"Oh, don't worry about it, Billie. Those are good memories—working with you girls. I enjoyed it."

Billie gave Dave his sandwich, and blushed a bit with a humble smile.

"Good to see you, Billie."

Dave Johnson has never seen Billie or Jenny since that chance encounter at Subway. But he still shares their stories with his college students today— two "rounders" who made his life miserable one hour a day for an entire school year. Yet, there was a culture of care that he had taken time to cultivate—however hard it was for the girls to show their appreciation.

Dave reminds himself that there are dozens of Billies and Jennys in any school—whether elementary, middle, high school, adult ed, college, or grad school . . .

And he realizes his most important responsibility with every student and every class is to care—not only for the technical aspects of the class and student productivity, but for the individuals in that class . . . many times traveling a long, lonely road.

CHAPTER SUMMARY

A veteran teacher recalls two students who created havoc much of the time in his middle school health and PE class. But he also remembers that he built trust with them—a connection that was more important than anything else he could have done to provide support for their dysfunctional situations.

QUESTIONS FOR REFLECTION

1. How many "lost kids" would you guesstimate are in your school?
2. What social and emotional training is provided for staff?
3. What are the barriers for teachers in providing daily individual attention and care for at-risk students?

FURTHER READING

Schultz, Q. (2022). *Servant teaching—Practices for renewing Christian higher education.* Edenridge Press, LLC.

Chapter 7

Rewrite and Repeat

Elisha Lawrence

"Many stressors invade a student's mind throughout their school years, but perhaps one of the most intensive for a child is the first day at a new school."

All people have four basic needs: food, water, space, and shelter. Unfortunately, for many students, their most consistent shelter is the one they receive when they walk inside a school building. And for some, the first day at a new school is a scenario that continues to repeat.

Elsa, the name that some called her, was a girl described by her former teachers as a daughter from a broken home who often shifted from one parent to the next. She survived her parents' divorce and was experiencing what her mom called "just one more move." The middle school she was moving to, during spring break, set her up with a guided tour by another girl her age, who appeared to be very kind and very knowledgeable about the school. The student's mom was an educator at the school, and Elsa thought this girl could be her first friend. The girl even remembered her name.

On the first day at this new school, Elsa's heart pounded as she walked alone to a large gym. No one told her where to sit, and no one greeted her to let her know where her class was, but she saw that girl. She went to her to ask what to do next, and the girl laughed at her. Elsa was devastated and afraid. She continued to go through the motions day after day, focusing on school work—the one thing she could control. Despite her routines, she often thought about what that popular girl continued to say each time she passed her in the hall with an entourage of friends laughing at her.

Elsa had no words to tell any adult about how she was being treated. She was the new kid, the outsider, and she thought no one would listen to her. There was no one to check on her to see how her days went, to encourage her, or to make her feel at home. Elsa felt alone, and she felt like she did not belong. Middle school continued to be rough but, thankfully, was short-lived. The transition to high school was at least in the same school district, so the first day of school felt somewhat better. However, it wasn't until her sophomore year that she met a teacher, Mrs. Wilson, who changed her perspective. She saw through Elsa's awkwardness and into her gift as a writer.

The sneers from peers continued through the years, but despite the words that her classmates may have used to harm her, Elsa found words, in contrast, to create an alternate world. Her writing was her solace, and she penned the hopes of better "first days." Mrs. Wilson, who took the time to invest in her, revealed to Elsa her strength in writing. And it was writing that allowed Elsa to alter the course of her future. Her words yielded the rewards of winning competitions and scholarships for college.

Mrs. Wilson allowed Elsa to find the potential inside herself to transcend time, which led her to become a teacher herself. This teacher, despite all the changes in Elsa's life, was a constant reminder of encouragement and hope. Mrs. Wilson took the time to inspire Elsa and celebrate her potential and success.

Thinking about Elsa's story, how would you, as her teacher, ensure Elsa had a better beginning if you had a chance to rewrite her story?

As an adult, Elsa's husband was called to ministry, which meant that her family relocated often. Elsa saw the cycle repeating because her daughter, Cadence, had moved eight times by the time she was twelve. This was not a path Elsa had wanted for her daughter, but as servant leaders, she and her husband thought that with each move they were doing the right thing. They ministered to thousands of students in various parts of their state throughout the years. Although their intentions were pure, as they wanted to serve, there came a time when Elsa was willing to do any job other than serving in ministry or teaching if it meant she would not need to move her family again.

Teacher cutbacks had hit Elsa's family hard. After giving up her tenure in one district to relocate for ministry, she found herself in a tailspin of one-year contracts. The administrators were hopeful and encouraging, as they would try to rehire her, but unfortunately, their district budgets did not always allow her to stay. Not being from the communities in which she served also made it difficult for her and her family to sustain connections. She was told time and time again, "Children are resilient!" but she believed there would come a time when the moving would stop and roots would be planted.

After Cadence turned twelve and was about to start middle school, Elsa plunged her feet deep into the soil of her community. She even took a massive pay cut, choosing not to take another one-year teaching contract but to embed herself into their new community completely. She was willing to do whatever it took to keep her daughter from having to experience another first day at a new school.

Thankfully, Elsa was able to keep her promise, and her daughter graduated high school in the same district where she started middle school. Cadence applied for different scholarships, and in one essay specifically, she shared with the reviewers about her multiple moves. She described her first days at each new school as opportunities to become another person. Depending on the friends she wanted to make, she adopted new interests, leading her to be a musician and an athlete. Thankfully, Cadence only had a few mean girl encounters. But Elsa recalled, in her daughter's words, the heart-pounding and alone feeling she felt each time she had a first day at a new school.

How much would Elsa have liked to have rewritten a different childhood for her daughter. Although she later reflected on the growth she experienced with each move, it grieved Elsa to know the pain Cadence had felt with each repeat of a first day at a new school.

Educators know the students in their classrooms and schools who are like Elsa, just passing through or only there for a short while. And they can learn to be grateful for every opportunity to share life with these kids, no matter their duration in the classroom or school. How can teachers help make a student's first day at a new school a positive one?

Consider these suggestions:

- In elementary school, significant identifiers exist for students who feel like they belong. One way to ensure a sense of belonging is by offering backpacks filled with school supplies. This simple gift gives a child who has experienced a lot of change and transition the opportunity to have something they can call their own.
- In all age ranges, partnering new students with peers and teachers to show them around for their first day can make all the difference. Children should not feel alone in what might be their closest thing to a consistent home.
- Sitting alone at lunch is a huge stressor for a student, especially on their first day at a new school. Be thoughtful of who they are seated by, as they should not experience their first meal in their new school feeling like they do not belong.
- Interest inventories can help determine who or what to connect students to on their first school day. These can be completed before their first day or as a quick questionnaire they complete when they arrive. Allow students to share their interests and past accomplishments. This sharing time will allow the student to feel like someone cares to know who they are. Then take their responses and find ways to connect them with opportunities to apply their strengths and enjoy future success.

- Socialization impacts a student's self-image and character for generations. It is only through positive social interactions that a student can be propelled toward their potential.
- Whether or not teachers have experienced these constant repeats of transition, they have the opportunity as an individual to walk alongside a child, to share in their growth, and to experience the revelation of the unique individual they are destined to become. Each teacher has this opportunity when they invest their time to help rewrite the story of a student's first day at a new school.

CHAPTER SUMMARY

An educator shares what it was like to move her child around a lot in the early days of her career and adds insightful recommendations for how teachers and schools can more effectively meet the social-emotional needs of new students.

QUESTIONS FOR REFLECTION

1. What processes are your school's staff trained in to provide a positive orientation and welcoming experience for new students?
2. How are the parents or guardians of these kids provided with helpful information when they first arrive on the first day of school?
3. What interventions are put in place for new students who are not settled in well in their initial days of school?

FURTHER READING

Wildenhaus, C. (2019). *Helping Children Manage Anxiety at School.* Self-published.

Chapter 8

Sometimes You Just Need a Little Push
Holly Kay Graham

"One lifeline, extended by someone who cares, can change a life—saving it from the bottomless pit of pain and abuse."

It was Beth's seventh year as a teacher. Even though she had only taught in public schools for a few years, she still had a lot of experience working with youth in other avenues. There was one student that impacted her more than any in her first years of teaching; her name was Sherri. Beth had grown up in Kentucky but had found herself teaching in rural Appalachia in Tennessee, a small mountain town where outsiders were not accepted.

Sherri came from a low socioeconomic level family in the small mountain town where Beth was teaching. Like a lot of the children in the area, both her parents were incarcerated for drugs, so she was being raised by her uncle and aunt. Because this couple was raising multiple children from different family members, Sherri was not a priority in their home. She was often neglected.

Sherri was in Beth's eighth grade homeroom, and Beth was excited and ready to tackle another year of eighth grade English Language Arts. In fact, she was always excited at the beginning of a new school year. She had a plan of action for procedures and discipline and shared it with her students. But within the first few weeks of school, she knew her homeroom was different. The kids did not want to listen, participate, or follow directions. Beth knew she had her hands full that year. Discipline would be a hurdle with this group of students, but she would make due.

One of Beth's students, named Donnie, needed extra support for his behavior and tended to talk back and not listen. She was very patient most of the time, but sometimes his smart mouth and lack of respect was too much. One day, Donnie was picking a fight and wanted to argue, so Beth shut it down. Sherri jumped in and told Donnie to shut up. A small argument happened as he didn't stop. The incident went further as Sherri said she would beat him up if he didn't leave Ms. Beth alone. From that day on Sherri and Beth began a teacher-student friendship that continued into the school year.

Sherri oftentimes would come into school very distraught from the night before. She didn't completely want to share what was going on, but Beth knew deep down that she was having a hard time, and it rooted from home. She talked to the child daily, and Sherri came to Beth's room when she needed to talk about random things. Beth was concerned for Sherri, but she wasn't sure about what was going on at home and didn't pry.

As the two developed the mentor-mentee relationship, a crisis happened in Sherri's family one afternoon. One of Sherri's cousins, a niece, had been accidentally hit by a grandparent in their driveway, and the little girl died. Beth knew after hearing about this tragedy that Sherri was going to be upset and wasn't sure when she would be back at school because of the death.

The next day, Sherri was at school. She was forced to attend because her family was quite large and her staying home for the day was not an option. Beth knew she needed to help her get through the trauma of being with classmates so soon after such a horrific accident. There was a Bible study in Beth's classroom each morning that was open to all students. Sherri attended and cried the entire time. Beth asked her to go into the hall and talk. That day, Beth's relationship with Sherri grew even stronger.

Beth felt she needed to go to the funeral home for visitation and to provide Sherri support. She didn't want to go, as it was the most depressing atmosphere. When she got to the funeral home, she found Sherri, and they walked through the procession to see the small child in the casket. It was very hard, but Beth knew she needed to be there for her student.

As the years went by, Beth continued to check on Sherri as she went to high school. It was harder to talk to her because her aunt and uncle were quite put off by a teacher becoming an advocate for Sherri. Sherri would often text Beth to keep her updated on her life and how high school was going. Then one day, she shared information that stopped Beth in her tracks. Sherri informed her that her uncle was "beating" her every day. Upon further questioning, Beth realized that the girl was truly being abused. As a teacher, she knew she needed to report this to social services, so she did.

The proper authorities checked on the situation, but the aunt knew the worker who investigated and informed her that there was no abuse going on in the house, so the case was closed. Beth sent another anonymous tip to social services, and once again it was ignored. She knew that she needed to do something for the student, even asking her husband if they could help. He agreed. Beth knew nothing was getting done, so she prayed about what she and her husband could do.

As Sherri continued to reach out, Beth knew the girl needed to get out of the dangerous environment she was in. When she was away from the house, she would text or call. Her aunt and uncle did not want Beth to talk to her anymore because they suspected that she was the one who reported the abuse.

Sherri and Beth thus had limited conversations. They tried to come up with a solution by communicating when Sherri was away from the house. As much as Beth wanted to just rescue the girl and allow her to come live with her and her husband, that was not the answer. But one day Sherri spoke of another aunt and uncle in Georgia who would often take her and her siblings for the summer.

This aunt and uncle did not have any children and treated the girls as their own. Beth immediately told Sherri to reach out to them and share what was going on. As soon as she opened up, her aunt from Georgia drove to Tennessee to take Sherri back with her to Georgia. This was very hard for Sherri, but Beth assured her that she had a better chance in life as time went on if she lived with her family in Georgia.

Sherri's family in Tennessee was livid; they did not want her to leave. Maybe it was the financial support she provided by working part-time jobs that Beth never knew about. But that day, Sherri moved to Georgia and left everything behind. This was hard on her because she didn't know anything else but the life she had lived in Tennessee. Yet Beth assured her that this was the best option.

Time passed, and after Sherri graduated from high school, she went to trade school and now lives on her own. She has a good full-time job and is able to support herself as an adult. She sometimes visits her family in Tennessee but keeps these trips brief.

One day, Sherri sent a message to her former teacher, Beth, thanking her for never giving up on her and helping guide her to her aunt and uncle in Georgia. She said that it was one of the hardest things she had ever done but she wouldn't be where she is today if Beth hadn't taken time to care.

CHAPTER SUMMARY

A student from a low socioeconomic level family was being neglected and hurt by her caregivers. A discerning teacher stepped in to help her get the support she needed, even years after having her in class. The girl is now a successful adult who lives on her own.

QUESTIONS FOR REFLECTION

1. Have you had a "Sherri" in your classroom and not known exactly what to do?
2. How do you reach out to your students during a stressful school day?
3. How can you help these students be successful?

FURTHER READING

Jensen, E. (2009). *Teaching with poverty in mind.* ASCD.

Chapter 9

Connecting SEL to Mentoring for African American Male Students

Jeffrey Herron

"I've learned that people will forget what you said, people will forget what you did, but people will never forget how you made them feel."

—Dr. Maya Angelou

Education is impacted by many social factors beyond the control of school administrators and teachers, but due to a lack of knowledge, educators are often not prepared to educate African American students, especially African American males. Many times, students come from below poverty areas that lack the necessary resources. Urban schools are generally associated with high rates of poverty, limited resources, high population density, and lower academic achievement (Graves et al, 2013).

Herron and Turnley (2023) stated that school administrators should provide students with vital mentoring programs, family involvement activities, and activities that build strong relationships with the parents and teachers of the students. When thinking of what it takes to be successful in the twenty-first century as an African American male, one wonders if today's youth will be prepared to make a difference in society. Educating African American males has become a nationwide epidemic that involves many social and economic issues that play significant roles in the overall success and failure of the student (Herron & Turnley, 2023).

Over the years, social and emotional learning (SEL) has encompassed a range of programs and practices such as self-awareness, social awareness, and relationship skills or relationships in general within schools. According to Reyes-Portillo et al. (2013), these initiatives broadly aim to develop "social competence." A study by Graves and associates (2013) found that students in SEL programs have outcomes that suggest statistically significant increases in social-emotional skills, socially appropriate behavior, positive attitudes, and academic performance.

The development and implementation of SEL interventions are vital in schools. School-based SEL programs counteract common mechanisms of risk and foster the protective resources in all of three dimensions of educational resilience: The students themselves, their educational and social environments, and the interaction of these dimensions over time (Reyes-Portillo et al., 2013).

In addition, schools are lacking the systematic and coordinated efforts to meet the needs of those students who are at risk. Mentoring can be connected to SEL through the lens of relationships. Mentoring can take on many forms but generally focuses on academic performance, social involvement, and academic persistence (Dunn & Herron, 2023). Schools can offer mentoring programs to students, which can help the students connect socially and emotionally to themselves, their peers, and teachers.

Mentoring relationships can create an emotional bond, trust, social engagement, safety, affirmation, and encouragement with the mentee, which could lead to outcomes for success. An example of appraisal behavior is when a mentee is working diligently on an assignment and the mentor checks in on the progress of the mentee (Dunn & Herron, 2023). The mentor can also use active listening skills to help gain trust with the mentee, provide feedback to help modify the mentee's plan of action, and also help the mentee overcome obstacles (Dunn & Herron, 2023).

A mentor has the opportunity and responsibility to transfer knowledge, wisdom, and perspective to someone else who is seeking guidance, direction, and perhaps—acceptance. As a mentee, it is also important to seek out guidance and provide transparency about what skills or direction are needed in being helped to move forward.

A solution:

The local college funds a group or organization within the college called Together in Excellent Standards (TIES), which is a mentor program that is partnered with local high schools. TIES mentors are all African American males within the college, such as administrators, faculty, and staff. The purpose of this group is to help African American men with academic support, emotional support, learning techniques, and college prep, and to connect them with services within the community.

For students to be accepted into TIES, they had to be interviewed and have a GPA above 2.7. The program only accepted twenty-five students each year. In addition to the weekly meetings, there were guest speakers throughout the school year discussing different topics. At the end of each academic year, the program would celebrate those graduating.

CHAPTER SUMMARY

Many researchers consider SEL as important as academic content and believe it should be taught, modeled, practiced, and reinforced when working with students. In addition, African American male students and folks from lower socioeconomic backgrounds who are in or participate in SEL programs develop and strengthen their social and emotional competencies.

QUESTIONS FOR REFLECTION

1. What is your school doing to increase SEL for minority students?
2. What are you providing for the minority males to help them better connect with the school community?
3. Has your school administration and staff been thoroughly trained on the research in the domain of social emotional learning?

REFERENCES

Dunn, B., & Herron, J. (2023). Understanding mentoring in higher education. In J. Herron (Ed.), *Using self-efficacy for improving retention and success of diverse student populations*. IGI Global.

Graves, S., Herndon-Sobalvarro, A., Nichols, K., Aston, C., Ryan, A., Blefari, A., Schutte, K., Schachner, A., Vicoria. L., & Prier, D. (2017). Examining the effectiveness of a culturally adapted social-emotional intervention for African American males in an urban setting. *School Psychology Quarterly, 32(1)*:62–74.

Herron, J. D., & Turnley, B. (2023). Mentoring: Bridging the gap for African American male student success. In J. Herron (Ed.), *Using self-efficacy for improving retention and success of diverse student populations*. IGI Global.

Reyes-Portillo, J., Elias, M., Parker, S., & Rosenblatt, J. (2013). Promoting educational equity in disadvantaged youth: The role of resilience and social-emotional learning. In S. Goldstein & R. Brooks (Eds.), *Handbook of resilience in children*. Springer.

Part III

From a Parent's Perspective

Chapter 10

Love Covers All

Jane Bragg

"To be genuine includes showing unconditional love to those who feel less fortunate."

Teaching in the moderate to severe disabilities (MSD) classroom is both rewarding and challenging. The students who are placed in this learning environment have a variety of both physical and moderate to severe intellectual challenges. With this vast variety of disabilities in one classroom, one can imagine the tensions that may arise for those who perceive they have been misplaced in their educational setting.

Sam was a freshman in high school who had been in the regular education classroom setting for his entire formal school career. When he enrolled in high school, he was evaluated for special education. (Why he had not been evaluated earlier in his school career was perplexing.) After the evaluation and looking through past school records, it was determined that Sam's least restrictive education setting would be in the MSD classroom. Upon the initial meeting for placement, both the student and caregivers were distraught.

His grandfather (and primary caregiver) was concerned that Sam would not graduate with a regular diploma and that he would not amount to anything; he was also concerned about Sam's ability to acquire gainful employment and a driver's license. Sam resounded the same sentiments as his grandfather, with the additional concern of being negatively labeled and being with other students with more profound disabilities. He was furious and bitter about the new classroom setting he would be a part of through his high school years.

During the first few weeks of high school, Sam was extremely defiant and displayed aggressive behaviors in his new setting. He felt out of place and that he was a victim of injustice for being placed in the MSD classroom. As time passed, his teacher, Mrs. Arrington, began to "win" Sam over. Sam was a great artist. Anytime instruction involved artistry, he was eager to draw. Being one of the top students in the classroom, he eventually became a helper to the less functioning students. He knew Mrs. Arrington cared for him personally and cared about his success. She knew how important it is for students to know their teachers care about them in the school setting and outside of school.

Outside of school, Mrs. Arrington became the coach for Top Soccer, an event for special needs students. Sam became one of the referees in the soccer games, and thus Mrs. Arrington had the opportunity to bond with Sam's family. Building a good relationship with his family assisted in increasing Sam's success in the classroom. He was beginning to feel comfortable at school and was becoming a successful student. Then, suddenly, he became angry and bitter again.

Mrs. Arrington made a home visit, as she had done previous times, and discovered Sam's grandmother was diagnosed with cancer. The family was devastated, and Sam had trouble handling the news. Mrs. Arrington decided to bring the family a meal once a week. As time went on, she and her girls devotedly prepared numerous meals each week. The family was very grateful. During these times, Mrs. Arrington was able to provide support for Sam and his family. If the family needed anything, she was there to help them. She began to provide extra academic support to Sam and his younger sibling too. She was a welcome sight to a family.

The grandfather now believed that his teacher had Sam's best interest at heart and that she believed he was going to be a productive citizen in society as an adult. And Mrs. Arrington began to learn more about Sam's strengths and interests outside of class. For example, he was very interested in cars. So, for his last year of high school (at the age of twenty-one), she found him volunteering at a car shop. Sam was able to spend half the day there during school hours. This valuable time allowed him to gain experience in auto repair. After graduation, he continued working at the car shop in a paid position. Even though Sam graduated with an alternate high school diploma, he was able to gain employment in a field he was passionate about.

Since graduation, Sam's grandparents have both passed away. He was able to marry his high school sweetheart, and the couple has two beautiful girls. Sam remains working at the auto shop.

CHAPTER SUMMARY

Sam was a student who fell through the cracks in education until he reached high school. He was angry and defiant after suddenly being placed in a special education setting. As time passed, he began to excel in school and became a leader in the classroom. Unconditional love both in and outside of school by his special education teacher taught Sam the meaning of trust and relationships. He went on to be successful in his adult life.

QUESTIONS FOR REFLECTION

1. How many students in your school do you estimate were not diagnosed and properly placed in their least restrictive environment at an early age?
2. What social and emotional learning training is provided for special education teachers?
3. How can special education teachers provide opportunities for social and emotional learning in the classroom?

FURTHER READING

Hoerr, T. P. (2020). *Taking social emotional learning schoolwide.* ASCD.

Chapter 11

Through the Eyes of a Parent

The Other Side of the Table

Laura Beth Hayes

"We need to dispel the myth that empathy is 'walking in someone else's shoes.' Rather than walking in your shoes, I need to learn how to listen to the story you tell about what it's like your shoes and believe you even when it doesn't match my experiences."

—Brene Brown

As Kair pulled Leah's chair back and sat down at the table, Leah knew what was coming. As a veteran teacher, she has sat in on many Admissions and Release Committee (ARC) meetings throughout her career. She fidgeted in her seat as she nervously awaited the discussion. Parent rights were shared, pleasantries completed, and introductions were made. This meeting was different for Leah, though, because she was the parent. Emotions escalated and words felt intensified because Leah knew hard conversations needed to take place. It is never easy to discuss the shortcomings or poor behavior observed by others when it comes to your child, especially when both parents are educators.

Kair, an international adoptee at the age of nearly three, was diagnosed with reactive attachment disorder just a few months prior. Despite the best intentions of his parents—valiant efforts, multiple forms of therapy, and an enormous amount of love—they simply had not been able to turn the behaviors around. Sometimes love is not enough. Sometimes all the knowledge in the world doesn't fix it.

As a parent, Leah felt such a range of emotions. She was thankful for options in the school setting to help her son, but she also felt embarrassment, shame, and disappointment. She was embarrassed that Kair had to be restrained, that she had taken him home numerous times because he couldn't finish out the school day, and that he melted down in front of classmates and

51

colleagues. She felt ashamed that she couldn't fix his issues and that, no matter how she tried, he didn't act like his "normal" peers.

Leah felt disappointment for her son, for herself, and for the life she and her husband had envisioned when they adopted him. He was rarely invited to birthday parties or included in social functions, and he was never going to win the coveted weekly or monthly good behavior and successful student awards. His issues created such a stressful home environment, but work had been Leah's escape. Now those issues crept into every hour of her day, to the point that she never felt reprieve or peace. She was as hypervigilant as he was, and that was only exacerbated by the sudden and tragic death of her own mother just months before.

Life in Leah's own mind was so hard some days, yet this committee didn't hear or see all of those thoughts and feelings on a daily basis. She was not sure that they would understand how hard each day was for her son and for her family. If they didn't understand the intensity of the situation, she felt they may not understand what Kair needed and worried they would be quick to judge all of his family.

As Leah tried to focus on the meeting, tears welled up in her eyes. Would they see her son as more than just data? Would they care about the fact that he lived in four homes before the age of two and that he was abandoned in a box by his birth family? Would they understand how hard Leah had tried and the countless nights she didn't sleep, worrying and researching a new treatment idea or plan? Would they approach decisions with a trauma-informed lens or would they simply think she hadn't disciplined him enough? Had they met about Kair (and her) prior to this meeting and formed their own conclusions and plans?

This meeting, to determine an emotional behavior disorder (EBD) placement, felt like a lifelong sentence and a label that Leah knew her son desperately needed and that she deeply feared. As the ARC team looked at graphs and intervention data, she spoke up and asked, "Can we talk about his early years? Can I share his story with you? Where we are at—in this moment—is based on so much more than data and what you see at school."

Leah was quickly given permission, and she poured her heart out, sharing her son's traumatic past and diagnosis. Tears continued to fall as the words spoke of the transitions in his life, being forced to learn a new language and culture, and the self-harm he had often inflicted on himself as a toddler. She shared about the nodules on his vocal cords from screaming, how he was in the hospital as an infant for weeks with no caregiver, and how he had night terrors weekly that were some of the most frightening episodes she had observed in a child. Students are not just data—they're these types of stories, these hard experiences, these uncomfortable conversations.

Thankfully, that day turned out to be a positive experience. Kair was placed in the EBD program, but he was given the chance to work with an outstanding EBD teacher who would prove to be an educator for his parents as well. She nurtured, equipped, and worked with their son during the day, listened to Leah, and allowed her to call her, weeping, in the evenings. Serving as his advocate, she trained teachers in his life in order to provide him with consistent support and love, so that the healing strategies she would teach him were reinforced in all aspects of his day.

When teachers failed to understand Kair's background or responded without his unique needs in mind, his EBD teacher intervened and fought for more appropriate instruction. She became a part of the family's lives and waded through the toughest years with them together. Most importantly, she loved Kair and saw all of him. She didn't just see the anger, the aggression, the inattentiveness, the manic behavior, or the sensory challenges. She saw a smart, talented, creative, and charming little guy who desperately wanted connections and relationships despite his inability to forge them or maintain them. She believed in hope, and she believed in her own ability to be stronger than his diagnosis.

As a school administrator now, Leah sits in on a variety of parent meetings. Every time she walks in the room, she looks at the parent and remembers those emotions, the tears, and the desire to be heard. She remembers that there is a story, a past, and a love for the child that may or may not be easy to manage or support at school. She remembers that the kids are more than the data or what may be written in a report. Social emotional learning (SEL) supports children, but it must also support and empower parents.

Educators are sometimes quick to blame a child's home life or situation. They may make assumptions about parental influence, what steps they've taken to help their child, or question their ability to parent the child as a whole. Often, they forget that trauma may have impacted the parent, too, and that the child's struggles often result in secondary trauma for the caregivers.

Kair is now functioning independently of an Individualized Education Plan (IEP), is on the honor roll, and was invited to participate in marching band as a middle schooler due to his "mature behavior" at school. His parents are so thankful for educators, like his EBD teacher, who understood the value of explicit SEL instruction, but also had a strong desire to empower and educate the adults in his life. Leah is a more empathetic, compassionate, and equipped educator because of the challenges she has lived through with her son. He has made her better, and she will forever be grateful for the day she sat in that conference room and worked through her own issues to better support her son and other children within my realm of influence.

CHAPTER SUMMARY

A teacher and mother of a child with significant social and emotional issues shares her own family's story and how it has helped her to be more competent at home and also in working with students at school.

QUESTIONS FOR REFLECTION

1. How are parents treated in meetings or in discussions related to trauma-affected students?
2. What efforts have been made to uncover or understand a child's past before dealing with anxious, unwanted, or problematic behaviors?
3. How can educators collaborate together to ensure that consistent SEL practices are implemented for a child in all aspects of the school day?

FURTHER READING

Purvis, K., Cross, D. R., & Sunshine, W. L. (2007). *The connected child: Bring hope and healing to your adoptive family.* McGraw-Hill.

Chapter 12

My Son CAN Read

Rocky Wallace

"Learning is not if, but how. Every child is unique, not an exact copy like others in the batch."

Zane was an inquisitive little fella from day one; mischievous, creative, cute, eager to push the envelope. All of these adjectives described him well—and these were only for starters. His parents and siblings doted on him constantly, and he took every advantage of being the youngest in the family.

As a preschooler, Zane's mom noticed he had some word enunciation issues and enrolled him in speech therapy. She herself was an early childhood teacher and knew the intervention would make all the difference. And it did. By the time first grade rolled around, Zane was pronouncing his words just fine. He loved school, and made friends easily.

But after a few weeks, his teacher was concerned and asked the little boy's mother to come in for a conference.

"Mrs. Simmons, we all simply love Zane. His antics and sense of humor, although extreme at times, make our classroom such an enjoyable and lively place every day."

Mrs. Simmons could tell there was a "but" coming. She braced herself, feeling the anxiety that she felt when being on the other side of this conversation with the parents of her own students.

"But we've noticed a delay in learning to read that is a bit alarming. Not drastic yet, but we think it's worth doing some diagnostic assessment soon."

"Mrs. Crabtree, I have worked with Zane on this. Obviously, as a teacher myself, I have stayed on top of it, and I am confident this is simply the typical delay little boys often have in their early years of schooling."

"OK, I tend to agree. I had also thought about the typical delayed learning factor. I'll keep an eye on it, and keep you posted." Mrs. Crabtree felt confident that Mrs. Simmons would follow up as needed with any interventions needed.

But at the end of year conference a few weeks later, both teachers were in agreement that something was not aligned.

"I am perplexed," Zane's mother shared in an exasperated manner. "He reads to me every night, and I read to him. But something's not clicking."

"And it's showing up in his other areas in class," added Mrs. Crabtree. "And I am noticing Zane withdrawing from his classmates. It's as if he's caught on that he's not computing as easily as the other kids."

Mrs. Simmons cried, and promised she would work with Zane all summer.

In year two, Zane struggled even more, and the relationship between his parents and the school plummeted. His new teacher vehemently blamed his falling further behind academically on his increasing discipline issues and felt he should be referred to the emotional behavior disorder program. But his parents opposed it, and a few weeks into the year, Mrs. Simmons took a leave from her own teaching and began homeschooling her son. Her heart ached, and she cried herself to sleep many nights, wondering why this was happening.

But one day, in a discussion with another homeschooling parent, she learned of a dyslexia center a couple hours away that had been having great results with kids sent there for intervention. She immediately set up an appointment to visit the school, and upon talking to the director, she was immediately sold on the idea of Zane going there in the upcoming summer.

The results were startling. Such a turn-around, in fact, that the following fall, Zane went to his mom's school as she returned to teaching. He was like a different kid. He quickly caught up with his new classmates and began to discover his passion—science and nature. His parents realized he needed more freedom to grow and learn based on his unique interests, and to have room to explore his thirst for all things outdoors. So, they took the plunge and followed through on a dream they had had for a long time—they bought a farm.

And, maybe not coincidentally, Zane went on to become an honor roll student at the top of his class. He graduated from high school with a 4.0 GPA and numerous awards and earned a bachelor's degree in agriculture from a state university, again with high academic honors. Today, he is a teacher with a master's degree in special education. And ironically, he works at an alternative school for students who could not make it in the regular school environment. He provides daily social-emotional intervention and care—still remembering well what it felt like to not be understood, as he began to drown in those early days of school.

CHAPTER SUMMARY

A young boy struggles in his early years of schooling until his parents find out about a learning center for dyslexia. Now equipped with the tools to cope with his reading disability, he goes on to excel in school, earns two degrees, and becomes a teacher who works with students who need intensive social-emotional care and support.

QUESTIONS FOR REFLECTION

1. Do you have a relative or other child in your circle of influence who needs extra emotional and relational support at home and school?
2. Does your school provide extra support to parents of students who have escalated learning and related social emotional needs?
3. Does your school have a proactive intervention process for students who display consistent anxiety or frustration during learning activities?

FURTHER READING

Johns, R., & Wallace, R. (2015). *Small handprints on my classroom door; Small handprints on my heart.* Rowman & Littlefield.

Part IV

School Administration

Chapter 13

Glass Houses

Ellen Hamilton-Ford

"What if each child lived in a glass house? This way teachers could drive by and see a small glimpse of the child's home life. But we don't live in glass houses."

The Harpers were an upper-middle-class family. As one third-grade teacher once put it, a Cosby Show nuclear family: a father, a mother, and two children (one boy and one girl). Every adult in the school building would mention "how nice the Harper family is," or "they are the perfect family." But what they did not know, which Ms. Thompson later discovered when she taught the oldest child, Lillian, was that this family lived in a dark, foreboding house.

How Ms. Thompson discovered the "going ons" in the Harper house came by way of Lillian's behavior. When Ms. Thompson was on morning greeting duty, she frequently noticed Lillian seemed to hate to leave her mother when dropped off at school. Ms. Thompson thought this could be due to anxiety, missing the mother, or even the dislike of school. When Lillian was in Ms. Thompson's first grade class, she cried inconsolably for thirty minutes after drop-off three to four mornings a week. The young teacher would hold and comfort her. After a while, the child would appear to be better and go about the day as if nothing had ever happened.

During class, Ms. Thompson observed that Lillian frequently did not pay attention. She was quiet, far away, or seemed to be daydreaming. When Ms. Thompson addressed her concerns with another teacher in the building, she was advised to share the information with the family and ask to have the child evaluated for attention deficit disorder. So, an appointment was set up with Lillian's family.

Mrs. Harper, who was most worried about her daughter, attended the meeting. However, she had no input about her daughter's behavior and was adamant that she did not want her evaluated. She stated that Lillian's unusual behavior was due to the recent death of a pet. She believed she was just sad or disappointed and would grow out of it. Ms. Thompson was a young teacher with little experience working with families and no children of her own, so she took the family's word and did not push any further. But she continued to watch the child suffer. Oh, what to do! She worried and feared for this child continually.

Several years later, when Ms. Thompson became a principal, she ran into the family again at school. Lillian was now in sixth grade. Her Individual Education Plan (IEP) stated she was diagnosed with learning difficulties for reasoning—organization and integration of ideas and thoughts—with the greatest delay in reading. In other words, the child could barely read. The middle school teachers wanted to know how she could have made it this far in school without being taught to read. Oh, but what they did not know.

Soon after, Mrs. Harper came to Ms. Thompson's office and requested a private conversation. The young mother confided that she was getting a divorce. She described in detail the spousal abuse she endured several times a week. She confessed that the children witnessed much of it. As Ms. Thompson sat crying with and for her, it was then that she linked Lillian's earlier behavior (refusing to leave her mother, inconsolable crying, and lack of attention/learning) to what Mrs. Harper endured.

Apparently, Lillian had been and was still afraid for the mother's wellbeing. Ms. Thompson knew that undiagnosed, untreated, or inadequately treated mental health problems can significantly interfere with a student's ability to learn, grow, and develop.

Mrs. Harper now sought advice on where she and her children should go for professional counseling or mental health services. At first, Ms. Thompson was at a loss. She knew of the community safe house; however, Mrs. Harper stated she did not need those services. Fortunately, the school had a trained mental health counselor on staff—not just a guidance counselor, but a person with a degree in counseling—who met with children during the school day when they or their families requested services. She discreetly gave Ms. Thompson the names of therapists in the area, also stating she would be available to meet with Lillian.

Fast forward several years later. Ms. Thompson periodically saw Lillian in the community, and she now had a family and children of her own. She once told Ms. Thompson that had she not begun counseling services at school, she did not know where she would be now. This comment left Ms. Thompson wondering: What if she had recommended Lillian to counseling services when she was the teacher? What if Lillian had access to professional interventions earlier in life? Would Lillian have been more on track to achieve her life goals? What if *all* schools, public and private, offered access to appropriate mental health services?

All children have the potential to thrive! Additionally, they are vulnerable to challenges they encounter in their experiences and contexts. Schools and educators committed to all students' well-being and academic success are examining their current practices and expanding their community's commitment to create the conditions necessary for all students to thrive.

While there is no one formula for creating and sustaining social emotional learning (SEL) environments, schools play a critical role as providers of mental health services—connecting children, youth, and families to counseling and mental health interventions. Early identification and effective treatment can make a positive difference in young people's lives.

CHAPTER SUMMARY

An educator recalls a child's survival of family domestic abuse and how, over time, she healed and overcame it with the assistance of school-based mental health services.

QUESTIONS FOR REFLECTION

1. How many children who witness or experience violence—watching a parent or other family member deal with an abusive relationship— would you guesstimate are in your school?
2. What school-based mental health services does your school provide?
3. Are school-based mental health services delivered by trained mental health professionals at your school?

FURTHER READING

Head Start Early Childhood Learning & Knowledge Center. (n.d.). *Preventing and responding to domestic violence.* Head Start. https://eclkc.ohs.acf.hhs.gov/family -support-well-being/article/preventing-responding-domestic-violence

Huecker, M., King, K., Jordan, G., et al. (2022). Domestic violence. StatPearls Publishing.

Office on Child Abuse and Neglect, Children's Bureau. (2018). *Child protection in families experiencing domestic violence.* Child Welfare. https://www.childwelfare .gov/pubPDFs/domesticviolence2018.pdf.

Chapter 14

They'll Be Fine, Kids Are Resilient ... Please Stop Saying That!

Franklin B. Thomas

"Suffering loss leaves scars. And when not tended to and nurtured, they can remain open for a long, long time."

The year was 1986. Jerry had just parked his car in the student lot at his high school and was walking toward the school with three of his friends. The previous evening, they had all received the news that a fellow student, Judy, had been killed in an automobile accident. All four classmates knew Judy to varying degrees, but Jerry knew her a little better because they were on the school's academic team together. The accident that killed Judy was particularly gruesome and disturbing. She had lost control of her car and slid off the road and underneath a large parked flatbed trailer. According to reports, the top of her car was sheared off, and she was decapitated.

As they walked, Jerry remarked, "I'm going to miss Judy. She was just in the wrong place at the wrong time, and bit the dust." The group awkwardly chuckled. This was an inappropriate and unhealthy way of dealing with the loss of a friend. In the group's defense, in those days, the school offered students no assistance in coping with the situation. The only acknowledgment was the principal requesting a moment of silence at the conclusion of the morning announcements over the school's intercom.

The story that has just been shared about a youngster struggling to deal with loss has a strong connection to social and emotional learning (SEL). This connection can be made through the lens of the popular "CASEL Wheel" graphic developed by the Collaborative for Academic, Social, and Emotional Learning (CASEL). This wheel depicts the key SEL concepts of self-awareness, self-management, responsible decision-making, relationship skills, and social awareness (CASEL, 2023).

Jerry needed to manage his emotions and behaviors more appropriately (self-management). To do this, he needed to recognize the emotions that he was feeling about Judy (self-awareness). He also needed to make a more constructive decision about whether or not his joke was appropriate (responsible decision-making). Finally, he needed to understand that his friends might be having a tough time dealing with what happened to Judy and show some empathy (social awareness).

More recently, the trend has been to offer students assistance and support in dealing with loss, such as the death of a classmate. For example, in 2017, in Arkansas, a fifteen-year-old student and member of the school band died in a motor vehicle accident. Their school provided counselors and pastors, had a memorial assembly and a flashlight vigil, and opened the band room for an evening of sharing memories about the student.

In 2021, in Alabama, a high school student was shot in the community. Their school made counselors and social workers available to the student's classmates. In 2023, in Illinois, a sixteen-year-old student and member of the school softball team died in a motor vehicle accident. The student's school memorialized her by having her initials embroidered on the school's softball team's shoes.

But is all of that really necessary? Aren't kids supposed to be resilient? Let's consider a few more stories from Jerry's life. Sixteen years after he cracked the inappropriate joke about Judy as he strolled into school, he found himself as the assistant principal of that very same school. As with many assistant principals, Jerry spent much of his day dealing with discipline issues, and students found to be smoking was one of the most frequent. A prolific visitor to Jerry's office for this infraction was Brad. He was a pleasant boy, but nothing short of a legend in the minds of his classmates for his exploits—smoking and otherwise.

Late one evening, Jerry received a telephone call notifying him that Brad had been killed in a speed-related accident. Similar to the situation with Judy a decade and a half earlier, the school announced the death to the student body, requested a moment of silence, and went on with business as usual. The school counselors may have spoken with a few students who took the initiative to seek help. Left to their own devices, a sizable group of Brad's friends decided to memorialize him in a way that they thought he would have enjoyed. At a predetermined time, they walked out of class without permission and gathered in the school's lobby, where they all lit a cigarette in his honor and in violation of school rules.

At that moment, Jerry had to make a snap administrative decision. Does he stay in his office and let the students' memorial event take place, or does he intervene? Whether his decision was right or wrong is certainly a point of debate, but he decided to intervene. At the very time that the incident was reported to Jerry, he happened to be meeting with the school resource officer (SRO), who was also a deputy sheriff. When the SRO realized that Jerry wanted to stop the students, he told him to go to the lobby, approach each student who was smoking one at a time, tell them to put out the cigarette, and that he would take over if they refused.

The two arrived in the lobby, and Jerry went up to the first student in the group and said, "Put out the cigarette." Sure enough, the student refused. The SRO then pulled out his citation book and filled out a written report accusing the student of violating a little-known state law prohibiting students from being insubordinate with school personnel. He handed the student the citation and informed him that his court date was at the bottom of the form.

The two men moved on to the next student, and the scene played out again in the same manner, and the same with a third student. Finally, beginning with the fourth student, the remaining students complied. They were told to return to class and were disciplined for leaving class without permission and smoking.

So, is all that we currently do to assist students in dealing with loss necessary? Signs point to yes. Five years after his experience with the student smokers, Jerry was the principal of a middle school in a different district. While traveling to a professional development session in another part of the state that had been required of all principals by the district office, he received a telephone call from his assistant informing him that one of his seventh grade students, Rhonda, had been struck by a vehicle while crossing a road the prior evening and had just died in the hospital.

The assistant said that he believed that he needed to announce the death to the student body immediately so that the news didn't arrive as a rumor. Jerry agreed, but instructed his assistant to be absolutely certain that his facts were straight. Jerry then called the district office with the news and asked permission to return to his school instead of attending the professional development session. He was told to go to the session and to let his assistant deal with the situation at his school. He complied, but believed that to be flawed prioritization by the district office.

When Jerry returned to his school in the early evening, he found that the situation had been handled well by his assistant and the district. A crisis team consisting of the school's counselor, counselors from numerous other schools, a psychologist, and other student services personnel had met with any student who desired assistance. Rhonda was not a particularly well-known student, so a memorial service sponsored by the school was scheduled for the next evening in lieu of an assembly with the entire school. Also, an artist-in-residence happened to be working at the school, involving students in the creation of a sculpture that would be a permanent part of the front of the school. The artist decided to modify the sculpture to be a memorial to Rhonda.

The memorial service was held in the school's gymnasium. Jerry and several teachers and students spoke. In attendance were Rhonda's parents, and several of her friends from the school she previously attended in another district. After the service, Jerry said a few words to Rhonda's parents and began his usual walkthrough of the building to be sure that everything was ready for the next school day.

In the rearmost hallway of the school, he encountered several of Rhonda's friends from another school who had gathered at her locker. Although no students from Jerry's school were around, he assumed that one of them had told the other students the locker number. There were some flowers and notes taped to the locker, which also made it obvious that it belonged to Rhonda. Although they hadn't asked permission to wander through the school, it was fine for them to be there, except that they were using permanent black markers to write various messages on Rhonda's red locker and nearby lockers.

Jerry told the students that what they were doing was not appropriate. They stopped and started walking toward the front of the school. He inspected the vandalism that had been committed to determine how he could clean it up before the next day, finished his walkthrough of that part of the building, and then headed toward the front to get some cleaning supplies and a custodian.

About halfway to the front of the building, Jerry encountered the students again. This time they were using the markers to write messages about Rhonda on a large section of the school's cream-colored, block hallway walls. This time, he escorted the students from the building. Again, no students from Jerry's school who had been offered services through a crisis team were part of the inappropriate activity. So, is all that we do to assist students in dealing with loss necessary? Signs point to yes.

Helping students deal with loss is probably best left to those with special training when possible. However, teachers and school administrators may find themselves in the role of assisting, especially when they are among the most trusted adults in a child's life. As a result, knowledge of a few basic strategies is important for all educators.

Most kids are aware of the concept of death, even if they don't fully understand it. In discussing death with students, it is important that specific topics are developmentally appropriate. This may include not sharing too many details but rather mainly just answering their questions. However, it is best to be direct and avoid saying things like their friend just "went to sleep." Also, a discussion of the afterlife, even if it's just to say that their friend will live on in people's memories, can be comforting (Ehmke, 2022).

Adults shouldn't be afraid to show their feelings and should encourage students to do so too. Students may feel depressed, guilty, anxious, or angry. They may switch between those feelings and appearing to be happy as a coping strategy. Methods for helping students express their feelings include sharing stories, looking at photos, making a scrapbook, releasing balloons, or planting a tree. It's best not to push students to attend the funeral, but if they are going to do so, someone needs to prepare them for what they will see and experience. Finally, kids find comfort in routines, so schools should return to a normal school routine as soon as possible (Ehmke, 2022).

CHAPTER SUMMARY

A school administrator recalls incidents of student death and offers wise suggestions on what to do and what not do in providing comfort and support to the classmates and other friends of the victim.

QUESTIONS FOR REFLECTION

1. Can you recall any time from your childhood when you experienced the loss of a loved one? What assistance were you given in coping with it? What additional assistance did you need?
2. What procedures does your school have in place to help students cope with the loss of a loved one? How could these procedures be improved?
3. How would you have dealt with the students smoking as a tribute to Brad?
4. How prepared do you feel to assist a student coping with the loss of a loved one?

REFERENCES

Collaborative for Academic, Social, and Emotional Learning. (2023). *What is the CASEL framework?* https://casel.org/fundamentals-of-sel/what-is-the-casel-framework/#interactive-casel-wheel

Ehmke, R. (2022). *Helping children deal with grief.* Child Mind Institute. https://childmind.org/article/helping-children-deal-grief/

Chapter 15

The Toughest Egg to Crack

Kalem Grasham

"There are generations yet unborn whose very lives will be shifted and shaped by the moves and actions you take today."

—The Butterfly Effect

Too many times in education, a school entirely focused on student discipline is correlated with being successful. "If those kids follow the rules and behave, we have a good school." Those sentiments are often shared by faculty, community members, and parents. The increasing pressure usually results in school and district administrators pursuing punitive actions against students instead of investigating and dissecting the core causation of the misbehavior. The pressure can suffocate a new school administrator stepping into a leadership role with a superintendent demanding punitive actions against students.

Mr. Jackson had been a special education teacher working in a highly structured program with students diagnosed with an emotional and behavioral disability teacher for ten years before accepting his new role as assistant principal. He was excited to begin his leadership responsibilities in a new district.

The school year started in a typical fashion as the superintendent met with the leadership team to discuss goals for the year. The superintendent, Mr. Allen, was a thirty-year veteran in education, serving in various roles, including the last eight years as the district's CEO. He had reviewed the previous year's suspension rate and behavior data. He informed the leadership team that a memo would be issued to mandate suspensions for students who were chronically misbehaving, and including to be removed from school. Mr. Allen told the group that the community and parents deserved to have an orderly school, and students would fall in line with his expectations for the upcoming year.

Mr. Jackson left the meeting fully aware of the superintendent's desires and started the school year with a bang by suspending multiple students daily. The most challenging student he had to deal with was George. George was constantly in the office for being disrespectful toward fellow students and staff. He was an explosive kid whose anger could boil over and ignite at any moment.

Mr. Jackson would often get into escalating situations with George, where the school resource officer would have to be present, ensuring safety for all parties. The principal was adamant about showing the student he was in control and would often taunt the kid by issuing suspensions. But George seemed to be satisfied with being suspended, which allowed him to stay at home and away from school.

After several months of this repeated cycle, Mr. Jackson reflected on his training and experience as a highly structured program teacher. He had listened to a podcast focused on meeting all students' social and emotional needs. The lesson was, "Every student is one caring adult away from being successful." Mr. Jackson decided he wanted to be that one adult for George. He knew there had to be underlying issues with the boy that caused him to act out. He felt ashamed that he had gotten caught up solely focusing on suspending a student instead of looking at support structures. So, he made a vow to himself to establish a relationship with George by getting to know him better.

George was highly skeptical of this new approach. He looked at Mr. Jackson with doubting eyes, just knowing this new strategy was part of a scheme to get him in more trouble. After all, just about every adult in George's life ended up hurting him in one way or another. He did not trust adults with authority, as his experience often made him feel let down and disappointed.

Mr. Jackson was made aware that the youth service center director, Lisa, had an established relationship with George. He met with her and requested a check-in/check-out system be deployed. The intent of this process was to ensure George saw a smiling and welcoming face at the beginning and end of each day. Plus, he really enjoyed talking with Lisa. The majority of the conversations would steer toward his favorite sports team.

One day during the daily check-in, Mr. Jackson dropped by to talk with George and Lisa. George reluctantly participated in a conversation with Mr. Jackson. He found out they both rooted for the same college football team and spoke excitedly about the big win over the weekend. Mr. Jackson sensed he had made his first breakthrough.

The very next day, George's juvenile justice worker showed up at the school to check on him. The worker was dismayed to see the multiple days of suspension and threatened to send the student back to court to appear in front of the judge. In front of George, Mr. Jackson started to praise his recent progress and asked the worker for additional time to prove George would get things turned around. George sat speechless as his principal turned into his biggest supporter and advocate. The juvenile justice worker agreed to grant an extension.

The next day, George approached Mr. Jackson and asked to speak to him in the office.

"I want to thank you for yesterday, as I was sure I was about to get sent off. I know I need to do better. It's hard at my house. I have two younger siblings, and I have to do everything for them at home. My mom struggles with drugs and lies in bed stoned every night."

George started crying as he opened up about his home life. Mr. Jackson looked at him to reassure that he was in his corner for sure.

"I know we got off to a rocky start. I am a new administrator and felt pressure to suspend students to prove my worth to the superintendent. I apologize that our relationship started so rough. Let's agree that we both will work to trust one another and speak openly about making you successful."

George stood up and shook Mr. Jackson's hand.

The principal proceeded to set up weekly meetings with the student to continue the positive momentum. George still struggled at times, but made huge strides when issues arose, and worked on de-escalation strategies to minimize his outbursts. Mr. Jackson continued to advocate for him with the court system and worked with outside agencies to provide additional support for the boy and his siblings at home.

George became the first person in his family to graduate high school. A tradition existed at his school where each senior was given an honorary diploma. The senior would then present it to a staff member who went above and beyond to help them be successful. George proudly walked up to Mr. Jackson and said,

"I want to thank you for believing in me and giving me a chance. You had faith in me when others didn't. I know I was a tough egg to crack, but I appreciate you caring about me and always being there."

CHAPTER SUMMARY

A principal feels pressure to increase his suspensions of misbehaving students, but changes his approach when taking time to get to know a boy from a troubled home. He begins to take the student under his wings, and the kid turns it around, going on to be the first in his family to graduate from high school.

QUESTIONS FOR REFLECTION

1. Is there a team at your school that regularly looks at behavior data? If so, do you include on this team the Family Resource Youth Service Center staff, counselors, and social workers?
2. Does your school provide training for all staff to identify social and emotional learning strategies?
3. Is there a relationship between the school and community service providers, such as the family court system and department for community-based services?

FURTHER READING

The Arbinger Institute. (2015). *The anatomy of peace: Resolving the heart of conflict (2nd ed.).* Berrett-Koehler.

Chapter 16

Trix Are for Kids . . . SEL Is for Adults Too

Franklin B. Thomas

"Leaders should always be learning too, and when they stop doing so, the organization and its people suffer."

Marvin was serving as an instructional supervisor in a medium-sized school district with aspirations of being a superintendent. To that end, he was taking superintendent certification courses at a local university. During a unit on working conditions in a course dealing with organizational theory, he participated in a group assignment during which one group member was to describe the factors contributing to the best working conditions of their career. Conversely, Marvin's task was to describe the factors contributing to the most negative working conditions of his career.

Unfortunately for Marvin, this was not going to involve reflecting on a previous job, but rather his current position. None of the other group members were from his district or knew him personally. This made the assignment a bit less uncomfortable and helped him to be very open. He was given a few minutes to think and make a few notes before his presentation.

Marvin started by saying that the mission of the organization seemed to be one of self-interest and scoring political points, as opposed to focusing on a mission about what's best for the students. He went on to describe the organization as one that claimed great transparency but actually practiced the polar opposite and kept as much as possible hidden. This included some puzzling practices, such as not providing job descriptions to employees unless they asked for them.

Marvin also described several troubling characteristics of the superintendent, including appearing bothered when an employee tried to describe an issue in detail and even cutting them off mid-sentence. He also recounted stories of the superintendent being concerned with very petty issues, such as the temperature setting of the thermostats in individual offices (even placing locking boxes over the thermostats).

Marvin recounted really liking his co-workers. Nevertheless, he described many of them as being jealous over things like minor differences in salary, and having a secretary assigned to them for the longest amount of time. He also described them as being uncooperative at times and skilled at finding ways to transfer their work, or the liability associated with it, to someone else.

Marvin concluded by sharing additional details about the superintendent, including an intolerance for employees making an error—even yelling and cursing at them for doing so. The superintendent also saw no issue with adding additional work to the plates of already overworked employees. Additional monetary compensation was sparse, with only lip service provided about how much the extra work was appreciated.

Lastly, there was little to no importance placed on promoting social interaction, work-related or otherwise. Collaboration on projects was viewed with suspicion as just unproductive socialization. Lunch breaks were watched closely to ensure they did not exceed the set time limit. And, sadly, there were no celebrations of holidays, birthdays, or other significant events.

During the discussion after Marvin's description, someone in his group suggested that many or all of the negative concepts that he had described could be improved with a focus on social and emotional learning (SEL). Marvin was too psychologically exhausted from exploring all of the issues associated with his current job that he just shook his head in agreement. However, he was really wondering how this could be the case since SEL had already been an area of focus in his district for a few years.

Baily and Weiner (2022) found that there are often major disconnects between school leaders' belief in SEL and their plans for implementation. They found that school leaders tend to focus on the development of SEL in others and not themselves, and that this may be because they do not want to develop SEL skills that may make them seem vulnerable. They also found that many school leaders only considered SEL for students and not related to their work with employees.

Baily and Weiner (2022) also found that school leaders well known for an intentional focus on SEL have their own definitions of many of the tenets of SEL. Several of these include recognizing and controlling their own emotions, demonstrating empathy, promoting collaboration, developing trust, using deep listening, considering the "people-side" of issues, and comparing organizational goals to available resources. This short list of SEL concepts does match up very well with the issues shared by Marvin. SEL is for adults (and school leaders) too.

A final point by Baily and Weiner (2022) is that there is a lack of emphasis on the development of school leaders' SEL by those who support these leaders. They are educated, experienced adults, and so they should have an inherent high level of SEL functioning, right?

Consider another story from Marvin's time as a district instructional supervisor. It was about 5:00 a.m., and he was jolted from his sleep by a telephone call. Such a call is almost always bad news, and this was no exception. The call was from one of the high school principals in Marvin's district, who was also a good friend. The principal said that she had just received news that one of her students, Cora, had committed suicide by shooting herself the previous evening. Cora was a young lady who was rather popular, a well above average student, and the starting point guard on the girls' basketball team. The reason for the suicide was unknown at the time, as no note was left. The principal wanted some advice about what to do.

Marvin was no expert at dealing with such a tragedy, but he did keep a crisis quick reference guide in his home office. He read several of the key points to the principal. One point of emphasis in the case of a suicide was to make certain that none of the follow-up actions could glorify what had happened and precipitate copycats. As the response unfolded over the next few days and weeks, Marvin felt that the school did a good job, especially in providing counseling services to students.

However, there was one action that made Marvin uneasy. The school had just completed the construction of a weightlifting facility that would be used by all of the school's athletic teams and the community. As a memorial, the new facility was named in honor of Cora. Marvin worried that this could make suicide seem to an unpopular student as a way to receive recognition.

About six months later, another tragic event happened at the same school where the suicide occurred. A student, Elise, was killed in an automobile accident when one of her tires blew out while driving on an interstate. Elise was not as popular as Cora, was an average student, and was the first chair flute player in the school's band. Again, the school did a good job in dealing with the immediate aftermath of the tragedy. However, Elise was memorialized only with a small plaque displayed in the band room. The difference in how the two students were honored bothered Marvin.

According to the Education Development Center and American Foundation for Suicide Prevention (2018), because youngsters have an elevated risk for what is termed "suicide contagion," it is very important to memorialize students who have committed suicide in a way that does not accidentally glamorize either the student or their final action. It is also emphasized that schools should aim to treat all deaths in the same manner.

The moral of these two stories about Marvin's experiences in school administration suggests that even though school leaders are educated and experienced adults, they don't necessarily have an inherent high level of SEL functioning.

Too often, there is a lack of emphasis on the development of school leaders' SEL by those who support them. Fortunately, there are many research-based resources and experts available. School leaders should accept that they need to take the time to utilize them.

CHAPTER SUMMARY

A school superintendent struggles with his own self-understanding of SEL, and thus routinely mishandles people and situations in his district. The research points to the need for more SEL training for school leaders, in addition to staff and students.

QUESTIONS FOR REFLECTION

1. What are some working condition aspects of your current organization that could be improved upon with SEL concepts?
2. Describe any experiences that you have had with an organization mishandling a crisis situation due to a lack of knowledge of SEL principles. What were the consequences?
3. Where could you turn to improve your knowledge of SEL?

REFERENCES

Bailey, J., & Weiner, R. (2022). Interpreting social-emotional learning: How school leaders make sense of SEL skills for themselves and others. *School Leadership Review, 16*(2), 1–33.

Education Development Center and American Foundation for Suicide Prevention. (2018). *After a suicide: A toolkit for schools.* Suicide Prevention Resource Center. https://sprc.org/wp-content/uploads/2022/12/AfteraSuicideToolkitforSchools-3.pdf

Part V

Personal Reflection

Chapter 17

Swimming Lessons

Joetta Kelly

"If we look outside ourselves for opportunities to help others, it will bless us (and them) in ways we could never imagine."

It's funny how a person can look back over their life and see how God put certain people there at specific times and for specific reasons. Sometimes the person doesn't really think about how they have been blessed by being a small part of helping God make someone's life a little better—until later, when they actually take time to look back and reflect. Some might call it a coincidence, but many Christians think there are no coincidences with God.

Very early in her teaching career, Miss Harlow remembered one such experience when she was a graduate assistant working on her master's degree, and teaching physical conditioning and swimming. Someone (she can't even remember who now) asked her if she would consider donating some of her time after classes to help a young student with a disability who was confined to a wheelchair. The student very much wanted to learn to swim, or at least be able to float in the water.

The young teacher remembered pondering on it for just a bit as she was new to teaching college students, having only taught younger children previously. But then she quickly said, "Ok." (As sometimes people do without thinking it all through or taking time to talk themselves out of it).

Miss Harlow met the student at the pool, and as she helped this young girl get into the water, it was discovered that *when she was actually in the water, she could stand!* The new teacher could only imagine how wonderful that must have felt to someone who could not routinely do that. She thought if it was her, she would probably never want to get out.

The two subsequently met several more times, and the teacher was able to help the young student float on her back as well as use her arms and legs a bit to propel herself. Later, when it came time to stand up, Miss Harlow thought through several options before telling the girl to do the opposite of what she instructed others in their lessons to do when attempting to float—because it would cause them to sink. She asked her to bend at the waist like she was sitting down in the water, because even though she had to hold her breath for a bit when she went under for just a few seconds, it would cause her to sink, and then she could put her body in an upright position. As a result, she would be able to put her feet on the bottom and stand back upright.

Other added benefits of the girl's time in the water were that it helped strengthen her muscles all over her body, including both cardiovascular and pulmonary muscles. But it also helped her increase her ability to do everyday things easier. The mental benefits were also great, as she increased her confidence, self-esteem, and feelings of independence. Seeing her smile more as a result was also a beautiful thing to behold.

Looking back at all the many students Miss Harlow has taught in the classroom, online, outside, in sports, and with students of all ages in the pool, she still reflects fondly on that specific swimming experience. Even though it began somewhat out of her comfort zone, it was an amazing time and still puts a smile on her face. She thanks God for letting her be a small part of His wonderful plan through this mentoring opportunity. The memory of this event also continues to enable her to be joyful and hopeful, and to always keep her eyes open for other opportunities.

CHAPTER SUMMARY

A teacher looks back over her career, and remembers a specific "moment in time" when she was asked to assist a handicapped student who could not swim. She agreed to help, and the results were pleasantly surprising!

QUESTIONS FOR REFLECTION

1. How many times have you been asked to do something just for the sheer purpose of helping someone who needs it, with no material reward in it for you?
2. How many times have you said yes?
3. How many times have you been so very glad you did?

4. Think of something you can do now for someone just for the sheer joy of making another person's life better. Will you do it?
5. What do you think about coincidences?

FURTHER READING

Chambers, O. (2021). *My utmost for his highest.* Our Daily Bread.

Graham, B. (2011). *Day by day with Billy Graham.* Billy Graham Evangelistic Organization.

Chapter 18

Performance Anxiety

Rocky Wallace

"If they only knew what is bottled up inside—but I can't get it to stop. So I just go on worrying and stressed, and do my best to not ruin it for others."

Bobby was a good kid, raised in a good home, and one of the privileged ones in his neighborhood, church, and school. He began playing baseball in the backyard with his dad as a toddler, and grew to excel in the game by the time he was in Little League.

When the youngster was twelve, he made the All-Star team and noticed an increased level of butterflies before he would play a game. He felt the pressure from the parents and community that this particular team was expected to go far—at least to the state tourney. He and his teammates did their best and won three games before losing out in the regional final—one game away from making state.

Bobby went on to play high school ball, but never completely lost the anxiety that would build up before games, and now sometimes throughout games. But his skills were good enough to land him a spot on his college team. Deep down, he wanted a break from playing ball. He had played every year since he was eight years old, and with the increased studies in college and other responsibilities, his ideal life would have been to simply hang up his glove and cleats, and relish the fact that he had had a good career with the game he had loved as a kid.

But his parents had invested a lot of time and resources in his childhood, and Bobby felt it would be running from the potential he had if he quit baseball at this pivotal juncture. So, he pressed on. He knew deep down inside that he could work through any mental block that was handicapping his performance.

But one spring day, about halfway through his junior year, and after staying up late the night before working on a paper, Bobby reacted slowly to a routine fielding play at first base, and was run over by an opposing player—breaking his cheekbone. The injury was serious, requiring surgery. Bobby realized his worrying and tentative play during games was at least partly responsible for this injury. This was a wake-up call. He determinedly returned to the baseball field the following year for his senior season, and never again allowed anxiety to control his performance to the extent it had before his injury.

But this young athlete and now young adult was left with scars, for sure. What if Bobby could have received proactive intervention that helped him control his nervousness leading up to and sometimes during games? What if he had had some training in how to cope with and minimize negative thoughts and stress during performance? Bobby noticed as he became a young adult that he dreaded public speaking and eventually gave up any type of sport—whether it be softball, golf, or men's league basketball.

The good news is that Bobby parlayed his training and experience into a successful career as a teacher and coach, and later as a school administrator, and eventually a college professor. He overcame his fear of public speaking and eventually even pastored part-time, delivered sermons every Sunday, performed weddings and funerals, and even gave a high school graduation commencement address.

Today, Bobby is a huge advocate for age-appropriate sports parameters and the limit of unnecessary pressure placed on young kids before they are ready to take on such responsibilities. He wears his scars proudly—as an overcomer. But he does still have the scars and always will.

CHAPTER SUMMARY

A young athlete develops performance anxiety and struggles with nervousness in the game he loves throughout high school and college. But he persistently overcomes his disability and learns to cope and even excel in areas of his life that require public performance.

QUESTIONS FOR REFLECTION

1. What are your school's intervention processes for students who show performance anxiety tendencies?
2. Do you have children or youth in your family or circle of influence who have performance anxiety issues?

3. Have you ever had physical side effects from the stress of public performance? How did you cope? How could you help your school address this emotional disability among your students and adult population?

FURTHER READING

Ankiel, R., & T. Brown (2017). *The phenomenon: Pressure, the yips, and the pitch that changed my life*. Perseus Books, LLC.

Chapter 19

The Mustard Seed of Teaching

Lisa Fulks

"Social emotional learning is the mustard seed of faith that must be planted in the hearts of students for them to grow both in their classrooms and in the rest of their lives."

"Catch this, Scarlett O'Hara," Mrs. Kemper said as she threw the eraser at Hope's friend. This may sound ridiculous for a second grade teacher to do, but she personalized her classroom by giving all of her students their own special names. She was full of fun. As a young student, Hope could not wait to get to class. She loved Mrs. Kemper, and Mrs. Kemper loved her.

Fast forward ten years. As Hope walked into senior English class and told her favorite teacher, Miss Hawkins, that she wanted to teach. She replied, "Well, alright, Hope. Grab my English book and you can teach my freshman class."

Hope was mortified, but more afraid of disappointing Miss Hawkins. So away Hope went and taught her first class, with her teacher watching and, of course, then conferencing with her about things afterwards. Mrs. Shively's belief in her student carried Hope throughout her teaching career, and her mentor remained one of her dearest friends and supporters until her death.

How lucky Hope was to have such wonderful role models of teaching as she grew up. They taught her that teaching was a lot more than academics. Teaching comes from the heart of the teacher to the heart of the student. Long before social emotional learning (SEL) education, these teachers knew the importance of the social-emotional connections with their students and between the students in their classroom.

As a young student teacher, Hope's knowledge of the importance of serving her students through social and emotional interactions continued as she met her supervisor, Mrs. Joyce Caudill, who looked and sounded like Cinderella's fairy godmother to her. She was the icing on Hope's teaching career.

She taught her how to love children toward their learning. She was honest and brought a passion for learning to each of her children in her classroom.

Mrs. Caudill turned her classroom into a rain forest when teaching about the topic. She played her piano for her children while teaching them to read through *Chicken Licken* and other short plays. It was such a joy for Hope to do her student teaching with her and then teach with her for the first fifteen years of her career.

The one thing Hope realized all of these teachers had in common was servant leadership. They truly served the students they taught as well as their peers, parents, and school communities. The first thing Hope thinks of about each of these teachers is how much they loved her and worked endlessly for her to be successful both as a student and a teacher. She remembers so many lessons they taught her because they loved her through their teaching.

Thus, as a young teacher, Hope knew from these role models that social and emotional learning would help her students be successful. She worked in an urban school district where children faced many obstacles and challenges that even adults would find difficult. Hope looked at her position as a teacher as a way to change lives and help students be successful adults in spite of the barriers. She wanted her children to feel the same love and belief that she had felt as a student, therefore each school year she strived to create not just a learning community but a learning family.

In the third year of Hope's teaching career, her principal said to her, "You work so well with emotionally disturbed and troubled students." From that time forward, Hope remembers being assigned every student with emotional challenges, along with every parent who had emotional challenges. Her principal began sending other teachers to Hope's room to observe and work with her, as well as student teachers to train. Looking back, whether it was kindergarten or fifth grade, Hope recalls that she and her colleagues did a lot to allow students to grow socially and emotionally. In a recent interview, she shared what a typical day looked like:

"I tried to start our days with joy and security to help students leave all of the bad that had happened to them before they got here. We began our day as students came in the door. I greeted them with a hug and a question about how their morning began. I tried to remember to tell them every day that they would do great things, and this is getting them ready for those great things. We would then go into a morning meeting to talk about what we were going to learn for the day, and they would tell me about what they wanted to learn.

Before starting our day, we danced together, as after such discussions we needed a brain break, usually using Greg and Steve or Hap Palmer songs. This only took 30 minutes, but it was what set the tone for our days. I used music for transition times. I loved to use the song 'You'll Be in My Heart' from the Disney movie, Tarzan. Students worked both independently and in groups for all content areas, and I met with small groups. Parents were encouraged to email their child a note during our language arts time.

Each week we changed into technology specialists to check emails during our work time, and then students would write their parents back. During our wellness or recess time, we usually played kickball together or acted out our favorite stories from the week. We worked outside under the trees when the weather was nice. We worked together all day, and students struggling in a content area were helped by their peers and worked with me in small groups. At the end of units, I asked students to show what they knew through stories, poetry, songs, reports, or any other way they chose. Then we had our pen and paper test.

On Fridays, we did reader's theater and experiments, and other creative learning. We cheered when someone was successful by giving mouse claps, alligator claps, ketchup claps, cowboy claps, baseball claps, and so on. I called the students mathematicians, reading specialists, scientists, and meteorologists to promote their image of themselves as unique and talented learners. I wanted them to believe they could do anything."

One day, while at the state fair, a young man yelled to Hope, "Hey, it's me—your worst student." Hope looked at that sweet 25-year-old face and could see the little third grader she had taught years earlier. He was not her worst student, but it was funny that he would say that. He said he was so glad to see Hope, and he just hugged and hugged her. Then he called his mom so Hope could say hello to her. She then talked to his mother, and then the young man told Hope all that had happened to him since third grade. How proud he was to tell her.

As he finished, he said, "You were my favorite teacher and I still try to do things that would make you proud." This was only one of various other reunions with former students over the years, and most of such encounters ended the same way.

When Hope thinks back to her beloved teachers and mentors, this is the same way she ended her conversations when running into them later, and the same way she thinks today. She still wants to make them proud. Pride is defined by Merriam-Webster as "reasonable self-esteem," or "confidence and satisfaction in oneself."

Yes, as an adult, Hope remembers her teachers. She does not always remember the content they taught, but she remembers how they made her feel. And the way she felt impacted her work in their classrooms and her work for the rest of her life (although she did not know it at the time).

The Wallace Foundation Report (2021) described SEL as teaching skills that people need to be successful in the classroom and for the rest of their lives. This is what happened to Hope, and this is what happened to the students she taught.

"For truly I tell you, if you have faith the size of a mustard seed, you will say to this mountain, 'Move from here to there,' and it will move; and nothing will be impossible for you" (Matthew 17:20–21).

CHAPTER SUMMARY

A teacher reflects back to her own schooling experiences as a student, and how her teachers connected with her in caring ways, and had such a positive impact. And, these mentors also shaped her own focus on SEL, and relational teaching and learning in her classroom.

QUESTIONS FOR REFLECTION

1. What school experiences have you had that shaped your teaching and SEL practices in your classroom?
2. What strategies do you use to embed SEL skills in your classroom on a daily basis?
3. How does your school encourage SEL practices in the classroom?

REFERENCES

Wallace Foundation. (2021). *Find out how to build social and emotional learning skills.* https://www.wallacefoundation.org/promos2/pages/navigating-social-and-emotional-learning.aspx?utm_id=go_cmp-827908937_adg-45169333809_ad-509434887038_kwd-375026528837_dev-c_ext-_prd-_mca-_sig-Cj0KCQjwtO-kBhDIARIsAL6LoreCvaItBEvoKuYE7kQK5lrO2j3QghyZind5T5hxFwD6JwOPFM710nIaAtpfEALw_wcB&utm_source=google&gclid=Cj0KCQjwtO-kBhDIARIsAL6LoreCvaItBEvoKuYE7kQK5lrO2j3QghyZind5T5hxFwD6JwOPFM710nIaAtpfEALw_wcB

Chapter 20

It's Just Not Fair

Marilyn Goodwin

"When we see through the eyes of the other person, we can then better understand what they feel when we're experiencing something we assume everyone else agrees with."

Maggie arrived at school on the bus, eager for the day to get started because it was going to be an exciting year in fourth grade. Mr. Bailey was coming today from the extension office for the first 4-H club meeting. As third graders, Maggie's class had watched the fourth through sixth graders participate and have so much fun with this club, and it was finally their turn.

The morning started off as normal. Mrs. Smith, the teacher, greeted the class and welcomed everyone to school. It was time to say the Pledge of Allegiance, and Tammy and Susie sat as they always did each morning during the Pledge.

These girls' families were of the Jehovah's Witness religion. They were not allowed to participate in the Pledge of Allegiance. So each morning they remained in their seats as the rest of the class stood up with their hands on their hearts, eyes on the American Flag, and proudly in unison said, *"I pledge allegiance to the Flag of the United States of America, and to the Republic for which it stands, one Nation under God, indivisible, with liberty and justice for all."* Maggie noticed both Tammy and Susie sat with their heads down.

Next on the morning schedule was reading. Everyone got into their small groups and started working on the reading lesson of the day. Then came recess. Maggie often spent time with Susie during the morning break, walking around the track, talking, and laughing. Recess was fun but ended too soon. The class went back inside and got ready for science, then on to lunch.

After lunch, Mrs. Smith informed her students that the special visitor would soon be there. Mr. Bailey arrived, and she introduced him to the class.

Everyone was excited about his arrival. Then what happened next had Maggie all confused. Mrs. Smith called Tammy and Susie's names and instructed them to go to the library. They slowly got out of their seats and left the classroom with their heads down and a sad look on their faces.

Maggie was wondering what had just happened. Why did her friends have to leave the class during the exciting time of the first 4-H club meeting of the year? It was hard for her to pay attention during the club meeting that day. Her thoughts kept wandering back to Tammy and Susie.

Every month, when Mr. Bailey came to do the 4-H club meetings, Tammy and Susie would be excused to go to the library. Maggie was sad that her friends could not stay and have fun with the rest of the class. Every time they left, she could see the pain and sadness in their eyes and on their faces. She had mixed emotions about 4-H club meetings. She was happy about the fun things but was always upset for her friends, who always had to miss Mr. Bailey's interesting lessons.

Maggie later found out the reason her friends were not allowed to stay during club meetings was due to their family's religion. Maggie's family was of the Christian faith, so she did not understand why the two girls were not allowed to participate in 4-H. The lessons the other classmates were learning during the meetings were all things to help students grow, and become better citizens. Maggie could not figure out what was wrong with 4-H that prevented Tammy and Susie from staying with their class.

As the school year moved along, it was time for fall activities in the fourth grade classroom. Halloween was nearing, and Mrs. Smith began discussing the party the class would have near the end of October. She would provide snacks and games for the party. The students were all excited.

The day of the party arrived, and everyone was ecstatic. Class started as normal with Mrs. Smith's good morning greeting, the pledge, reading, recess, science, lunch, and so forth. Later in the afternoon, it was time for the Halloween party. Mrs. Smith began to get the decorations set out and organized. Then it happened again. She called for Tammy and Susie to go to the library. They slowly got out of their seats, walked to the front, and exited the room. Maggie's heart sank. Why? Why did her friends have to go to the library yet again? Tammy and Susie looked so sad as they walked out of the classroom.

The school year was moving forward, and it was almost winter break. Mrs. Smith and Mrs. Davis, the music teacher, were planning a Christmas program. The fourth grade class would sing a Christmas song in the program. Mrs. Smith was also planning a nice party for the students in her class on the last day of school before Christmas break.

The day arrived for the program and party. The students had lots of smiles and laughter throughout the day. Some students, like Maggie, were nervous about the program but looked forward to it. Mrs. Smith announced that it was time to line up to go to the gym. All the students stood and lined up. Mrs. Smith then called Tammy and Susie to go to the library. Maggie was in dismay. Why did they have to leave their classmates again? Why could they not go see the program and sing with the rest of the children? Why were they always pulled out and sent to the library?

After the Christmas program, the fourth graders came back to the classroom. Tammy and Susie joined them and went to lunch with the class. Later that afternoon, it was time for the Christmas party. And guess what happened? Mrs. Smith called Tammy and Susie to go back to the library. Maggie felt really sad for her friends. This was the second time in one day that they were sent to the library while the class participated in fun activities.

Maggie felt it was not fair. She wondered how her friends felt as they left for Christmas break and had missed out on so much during the first half of the school year. What would their break be like? Would their families celebrate the holiday? How would they celebrate? Maggie pondered these things as she rode the bus home on the last day before Christmas vacation.

After Christmas break, as the school year progressed, the same thing happened over and over again. For the club day meetings, Valentine's party, and Easter party, Tammy and Susie were sent to the library while the rest of the class celebrated. Maggie always felt that just because of their religious beliefs, her friends should not be separated from all the fun activities. She believed it was just not fair!

Solutions:

- Create a system of substitute activity time that does not single out students when they are not allowed to participate in a school activity.
- Explain the reasons students are given alternative tasks. Don't simply leave their classmates guessing.
- Meet with the parents of students being denied school cultural experiences and work to find some middle ground. For example, may they observe play practice in the gym? May they remain seated and not have to be removed during customs that are not allowed due to religious reasons? And, can there be exceptions?

CHAPTER SUMMARY

A fourth grader is perplexed with how her school handles special celebration days due to the beliefs of two of her friends. Both girls are sent to the library during these special occasions.

QUESTIONS FOR REFLECTION

1. How do you think Tammy and Susie felt when they always had to leave the classroom during special or fun events?
2. How do you think this practice affected Tammy and Susie's social and emotional development?
3. How could Mrs. Smith have dealt with the girls' religious beliefs in a different way and not singled out Tammy and Susie?
4. How could the school administration assist in this situation?
5. How could Tammy and Susie's families have been involved?
6. How do you think removing Tammy and Susie from the fun events affected Maggie and the other classmates socially and emotionally?

FURTHER READING

Wildenhaus, C. (2019). *Helping children manage anxiety at school*. Self-published.

Chapter 21

He Deals With It

Deborah Holt

"It takes a village to raise a child."

—African proverb

As inclusive classrooms become the norm, as teachers are faced with a multitude of children who suffer from a variety of visible and invisible disabilities. Two of these disabilities are fetal alcohol spectrum disorder (FASD) and alcohol-related neurodevelopment disorder (ARND). Although similar to autism, they have their own sets of issues that affect not only the person who has been diagnosed with either or both, but everyone else around them. These conditions encompass a "range of physical, cognitive, and behavioral abnormalities" (Kable et al., 2015, p. 1) and affect the person's ability to learn and to care for themselves due to having problems with impulse control, short-term memory, social skills, and coping skills.

The number of children in the early childhood realm (ages birth to eight years old) who are being diagnosed with developmental disabilities and behavior issues is increasing. It has been estimated that 1 percent (1%) of live births fall in the category of FASD (Kable et al., 2015), with estimates of possibly 1–5 percent of the mixed-race population in the Westernized world, with even higher rates in countries with high poverty levels (Mitten, 2013; Paley & O'Connor, 2011).

Fetal alcohol disorders are difficult to diagnose if the information about the mother's prenatal alcohol usage is unknown. A child with a diagnosis of attention deficit hyperactivity disorder (ADHD) displays many of the same symptoms as one with FASD. However, the child with FASD does not respond as well to stimulant medications for ADHD as the non-exposed child (Kingdon et al., 2016).

The children diagnosed with either of these disabilities are plagued with maladaptive issues, including impulse control problems, attention issues, and poor judgment. Although researchers (Ase et al., 2012; Kingdon et al., 2016) do not agree on which skills are most compromised in children with FASD in daily living or social skills, they do agree that social skill incompetence becomes more prominent as the children get older.

* * *

Quentin Fletcher was diagnosed with FASD at the age of three; he is currently fourteen years old. He has two major diagnoses, FASD and ARND, along with thirteen secondary diagnoses including oppositional defiance, anxiety, ADHD, central nervous system disorder, and behavior disorder with mixed disturbance of emotions and conduct. His anxiety causes fear, and he does not handle transitions well. Socially-emotionally, Quentin is about four years old; chronologically, he is now fourteen. To the casual observer, he does not have any noticeable disabilities and can act like a typical teenager, as long as he does not feel overwhelmed.

Quentin's grandmother has custody of him, and his "village" includes an occupational therapist (OT), an applied behavioral analysis therapist (ABA), a US army lieutenant colonel (retired), a college professor, and the school system. He and his grandmother live with the professor and have done so for most of his life. This arrangement has helped with transitions, as he is constantly around the people in the household and can go or stay with any one of them without causing a disruption in his environment. Quentin has been in occupational therapy and vision therapy for most of his life, and he also has some medical issues that affect him. His therapies have been arranged to be at the end of the school day, and he always has a doctor's note for his medical absences.

Quentin attended school in inclusive classrooms for preschool and kindergarten. He was constantly in trouble and was sent to the office, causing him to miss significant blocks of instruction. He was home-schooled from first grade to third grade, but was enrolled back in the school system for fourth grade on the recommendation of the occupational therapist because he needed more peer interactions. His fourth grade experience was somewhat stressful. He did have an Individualized Education Plan (IEP) which supplied some support; however, the classroom teacher struggled with his attitude and maladaptive behaviors.

The school counselor, Mrs. Jennings, was an advocate for student success, supported Quentin, and helped him manage his behaviors. She and his grandmother texted every day, so both knew of his issues and worked together to help him feel supported. Mrs. Jennings told Quentin's grandmother about a school that was designed to take care of students like him. He attended there when he started sixth grade, and even though he was looking forward to it, he had major anxiety issues because of the transition.

During his fourth grade year, when he was feeling overwhelmed, Quentin could go to Mrs. Jennings' office and work on management techniques to self-regulate—some he was learning from her and some from his OT. This provided him a safe environment within the school. He made a couple of friends and maintained those friendships throughout the year.

He was still attending his therapies, and it was arranged with the school for him to be picked up right before the buses arrived so he could make his appointments on time. This worked well for all parties, as he was not missing any classroom instruction and at the same time was not getting caught up in the bus traffic.

Quentin's fifth grade year started on a positive note. Mrs. Jennings' office was his safe haven, and he almost enjoyed going to school. Things were going better for him, even though he still struggled with attention and getting his work done. But right before Christmas, Mrs. Jennings announced that she would be retiring over the winter break. Quentin was devastated. Mrs. Jennings introduced him to the interim counselor, Mrs. Taylor, but they did not have the same dynamic. She was not an advocate and made it known that she was the expert and did not need to be instructed on how to do her job. Quentin did not like her, did not feel safe around her, and would not cooperate with her.

The last half of the school year was miserable and very stressful for the boy. He no longer had a safe place, and he was forced to deal with the classroom environment as best he could. He still struggled with making friends, and his grades and his attitude at home suffered. Neither his peers nor his teachers understood his disabilities and were often mean to him. He was never disrespectful to his teachers, but when at home, he would have major meltdowns. He would scream and throw things out of frustration of having to cope at school. He and his home support team somehow managed to survive the year.

Mrs. Taylor did not approve of his being dismissed five to ten minutes early in the afternoons, and started counting the time against him. Between his medical absences and early departures, the hours added up. His grandmother received a subpoena to appear before a tribunal on truancy charges. She researched with the state education department and found documentation to support the fact that doctor and therapy visits (with notes) could not be counted as truancy. The school was given a copy of the report and reluctantly withdrew the truancy charges the day before the tribunal.

Quentin started at a new school in the sixth grade, with an amended IEP providing him even more support. The vice principal, Mrs. Edwards, struggled at the beginning of the year with some of the accommodations but soon became his strongest ally. She assigned a staff member to walk Quentin to class in the morning, and he could go to Mrs. Edwards' office when he felt overwhelmed. Middle school was still a struggle, though, not only because students changed classes seven times a day, but all of the students here had special needs—requiring Quentin to have to cope with their issues along with his own. By this time, he hated school and begged his grandmother to homeschool him.

Mrs. Edwards and the grandmother came up with a compromise for Quentin to attend a couple of hours a day (literacy and math), with the provision that he complete his other work at home. Then COVID-19 hit, and everyone was on non-traditional school status. Even with this new arrangement, the kid struggled. He was paranoid that the other students were staring at him, so he would turn his camera off. Focus was harder now that he was not in a classroom. With his camera turned off, he would be on the floor playing with his dog.

Thankfully, Mrs. Edwards arranged for him to have one-on-one instructional time with the math teacher and his life skills coach. The life skills coach also helped him with his other classes. He was finally progressing in his school work.

When face-to-face classes resumed, Quentin went back to school. Then he had a new crisis to deal with, as Mrs. Edwards retired. He again pleaded with his grandmother to homeschool him. She finally agreed to do so for the remainder of the school year, but it was still a struggle for him. Without a scheduled time to be on the computer, he always had excuses for why he could not do his work.

When Quentin went back to school at the beginning of the ninth grade, he no longer had his support system in place. The new assistant principal decided that Quentin needed to "learn how to be an adult," even though he was not capable of doing so. He is now part of a homeschool program through the county school system. He has a support coach and works on one subject at a time. His grades have improved through this program, even though his reading comprehension is still weak.

When school starts again in the fall, Quentin will be in yet another setting—a magnet school that offers the Junior Reserve Officer Training Corps (Jr ROTC) program. He is interested in joining the army, and he does well in structured environments. Maybe, just maybe, through the ROTC program, he will feel like he belongs.

* * *

Every child has the right to a free and public education in an atmosphere that is conducive to learning and, at the same time, provides a safe environment for everyone. School counselors, administrators, and teachers are responsible for creating this arena for all students, not just the typically developing children who fit into the ideal mold. Inconsistencies within schools, not just in districts, lead to inadequate support that some students require to be successful. There is no one-size-fits-all when it comes to a child's education. Sometimes things get accomplished by trial and error, but the bottom line is to support the student to be the best they can be.

CHAPTER SUMMARY

The research on children with FASD reveals they often need customized intervention support in learning to function effectively in daily life. An example of the struggles with school experienced by a boy who suffers from this disorder is illustrated, pointing to the need for schools to provide comprehensive care to students who are on the FASD spectrum.

QUESTIONS FOR REFLECTION

1. Since a school system is part of a "village," what can be done to strengthen the relationships between schools and parents or guardians, including those of children with disabilities?
2. Staffing transitions will happen in a school system every school year. What can be done to ensure the protocols of intervention and support for students with special needs do not change when the hierarchy changes?
3. Does your school or district provide a well-developed support system for students and employees who are victims of alcoholism in some way?

REFERENCES

Ase, F., Ilona, A.-R., Mirjam, K., Pekka, S., Eugene, H. H., Sarah, M. N., et al. (2012). Adaptive behaviour in children and adolescents with foetal alcohol spectrum disorders: A comparison with specific learning disability and typical development. *Eur Child Adolese Psychiatry, 21,* 221–231.

Kable, J. A., Taddeo, E., Strickland, D., & Coles, C. D., (2015). Community translation of the Math Interactive Learning Experience Program for children with FASD. *Research in Developmental Disabilities, 39*, 1–11.

Kingdon, D., Cardoso, C., & McGrath, J. J. (2016). Research Review: Executive function deficits in fetal alcohol spectrum disorders and attention-deficit/hyperactivity disorder – A meta-analysis. *The Journal of Child Psychology and Psychiatry, 57(2)*, 116–131.

Mitten, H. R. (2013), Evidence-based practice guidelines for Fetal Alcohol Spectrum Disorder and literacy and learning, *International Journal of Special Education, 28(3)*, 44–57.

Paley, B., & O'Connor, M. J. (2011). Behavioral interventions for children and adolescents with Fetal Alcohol Spectrum Disorders. *Alcohol Research and Health, 34(1)*, 64–75.

Chapter 22

Closing Thoughts

Rocky Wallace

Social emotional learning (SEL) . . . The term has exploded on the education landscape in recent years, and sadly, the SEL movement is often mis-
understood. In reality, SEL boils down to one core value litmus test: Are we
providing the appropriate support to meet the individual needs of *all* of the
students entrusted to our care?

If so, then kudos to those educators and schools who are doing this well.
Because, the bottom line is—this is why we have "school." It's not just a rite
of passage for our youngsters. It's not just the cultural tradition that many of
us remember as "the good old days." Instead, it's a lifeline for every child
we serve.

SEL is then not so much a "program" as it is a determined and educated
effort to make a positive impact on students who perhaps, at no fault of their
own, were dealt poor odds to navigate through life successfully, wondering
how they're going to make it day by day in a system too often designed with
a "survival of the fittest" mentality.

These kids deserve the best care possible, as well as to be loved and appreciated with the same passion we have for the star athletes, the star academics,
and the kids who have so much support from day one they can do well in life
without even going to traditional school.

Who are these SEL students? They're from all backgrounds. They suffer
from an array of disabilities and harmful tendencies. . . . From various types
of mental health and anxiety issues to child abuse, from being victims of
parents who are addicted to alcohol and other drugs to disorders brought on
by a chemical deficiency, from toxic relationships to poverty, from suicidal
tendencies to growing up in an often unstable society—the youth of the
twenty-first century struggle in unique ways (and yes, even the star athletes
and intellectual elites—privilege does not prevent SEL needs).

But there's hope. In these pages, we find an array of inspiring stories of mentors and advocates intervening in the life of a student and making a difference—sometimes in profound ways. And many of these experiences happened several years ago, but the impact lives on!

Servant leaders are those who embrace the reality that before a school is a true learning center, it must relentlessly create for all of its students a "culture of care."

Afterword

Dr. Marvin Berkowitz, co-chair of the Center for Character and Citizenship at the University of Missouri, once shared that one of the most influential variables in human development is social relationships. This especially applies to the emotionally sustaining qualities of a relationship and is the root of why students seek a sense of belonging among their classmates and teachers. For many students, the need to belong is manifested most by an absence in their life, rather than by a presence. For these, feeling connected is an arduous journey. And, where they are in their social-emotional development plays a big role in how quickly they will feel a true sense of belonging.

This is where the teacher and student's journeys intersect, and the challenges students face are often difficult. Sometimes, as teachers, we overlook this reality. With the advent of social media, the essence of childhood and youth has changed significantly over the past two decades. This is especially true when considering the social-emotional development of our students. A teacher's role in leading students in their emotional formation will be paramount. Teachers must embrace the reality that their role has expanded to include one of mentor, advisee, confidant, role model, and coach. Your ability to serve each of these roles in a positive manner will make a difference in the lives of many of your students.

This book, *Social Emotional Learning and Servant Leadership: True Stories from the Classroom,* is a simple but must-read for any educator willing to educate the whole child—academically, socially, and emotionally. Each story is true and is the experience of a teacher in the classroom, just like you. Nothing is contrived. Each story provides an interesting dilemma for the educator and helps give a better understanding of the complexities of serving in a classroom or school building in general. This book has the ability to serve as a powerful resource for those who look to go beyond simply providing for students to being an inspiration.

Dr. Mike Hylen
Coordinator of Department of Education
Southern Wesleyan University

References

Al-Fudail, M., & Mellar, H. (2008). Investigating teacher stress when using technology. *Computers & Education, 51,* 1103–1110. doi:10.1016/j.compedu.2007.11.004

Ankiel, R., & T. Brown (2017). *The phenomenon: pressure, the yips, and the pitch that changed my life.* Perseus Books, LLC.

The Arbinger Institute (2015). *The anatomy of peace: Resolving the heart of conflict (2ⁿᵈ edition).* San Francisco: Berrett-Koehler.

Ase, F., Ilona, A.-R., Mirjam, K., Pekka, S., Eugene. H.H., Sarah, M.N., et al. (2012). Adaptive behaviour in children and adolescents with foetal alcohol spectrum disorders: A comparison with specific learning disability and typical development. *Eur Child Adolese Psychiatry, 21,* 221-231.

Bailey, J., & Weiner, R. (2022). Interpreting social-emotional learning: How school leaders make sense of SEL skills for themselves and others. *School Leadership Review, 16*(2), 1-33.

Chambers, O. (2021). *My utmost for His highest.* Our Daily Bread.

Collaborative for Academic, Social, and Emotional Learning. (2023). *What is the CASEL framework?* https://casel.org/fundamentals-of-sel/what-is-the-casel -framework/

Collaborative for Academic, Social, and Emotional Learning. (2023). *What is the CASEL framework?* https://casel.org/fundamentals-of-sel/what-is-the-casel-framework/#interactive-casel-wheel

Collie, R. J., Shapka, J. D. & Perry, N. E. (2012). School climate and social–emotional learning. *Journal of Educational Psychology, 104* (4), 1189-1204. doi: 10.1037/a0029356.

Committee for Children. (2021). *Second Step K–grade 5 resiliency activities.* https://cfccdn.blob.core.windows.net/static/pdf/free-sel-resources/second-step-free -resources-gk-g05-covid-resilience-activities.pdf

Craemer, M. (2020). *Emotional intelligence in the workplace.* Rockridge Press.

De Nobile, J., & McCormick, J. (2005). Job satisfaction and occupational stress in Catholic primary schools. Paper presented at the annual conference of the Australian Association for Research in Education, Sydney, Australia.

Dunn, B. & Herron, J. (2023). Understanding mentoring in higher education. In J. Herron (Ed.), *Using self-efficacy for improving retention and success of diverse student populations*. IGI Global.

Education Development Center and American Foundation for Suicide Prevention. (2018). *After a suicide: A toolkit for schools*. Suicide Prevention Resource Center. https://sprc.org/wp-content/uploads/2022/12/AfteraSuicideToolkitforSchools-3.pdf

Ehmke, R. (2022). *Helping children deal with grief*. Child Mind Institute. https://childmind.org/article/helping-children-deal-grief/

Glasser, W. (1999). *Choice theory: A new psychology of personal freedom*. HarperPerennial.

Gosner, S. (2020). Good teaching is not just about the right practices. *Edutopia*. https://www.edutopia.org/article/good-teaching-not-just-about-right-practices/

Graham, B. (2011). *Day by day with Billy Graham*. Billy Graham Evangelistic Organization.

Graves, S., Herndon-Sobalvarro, A., Nichols, K., Aston, C., Ryan, A., Blefari, A., Schutte, K., Schachner, A., Vicoria. L., & Prier, D. (2017). Examining the effectiveness of a culturally adapted social-emotional intervention for African American males in an urban setting. *School Psychology Quarterly, 32(1)*:62-74.

Head Start Early Childhood Learning & Knowledge Center. (n.d.). *Preventing and responding to domestic violence*. Head Start. https://eclkc.ohs.acf.hhs.gov/family-support-well-being/article/preventing-responding-domestic-violence

Herron, J. D. & Turnley, B. (2023). Mentoring: Bridging the gap for African American male student success. In J. Herron (Ed.), *Using self-efficacy for improving retention and success of diverse student populations*. IGI Global.

Hoerr, T.P. (2020). *Taking social emotional learning schoolwide*. ASCD.

Huecker, M., King, K., Jordan, G., et al. (2022). *Domestic violence*. StatPearls Publishing.

Hylen, M.G. (2022). *The 5 habits of the emotion coach*. Rowman & Littlefield.

Jennings, P. A., & Greenberg, M. T. (2009). The prosocial classroom: Teacher social and emotional competence in relation to student and classroom outcomes. *Review of Educational Research, 79*, 491–525. doi:10.3102/0034654308325693

Jensen, E. (2009). *Teaching with poverty in mind*. ASCD.

Johns, R., & R. Wallace. (2015). *Small handprints on my classroom door; Small handprints on my heart*. Rowman & Littlefield.

Kable, J.A., Taddeo, E., Strickland, D., & Coles, C.D., (2015). Community translation of the Math Interactive Learning Experience Program for children with FASD. *Research in Developmental Disabilities, 39*, 1-11

Kingdon, D., Cardoso, C. and McGrath, J.J. (2016). Research Review: Executive function deficits in Fetal Alcohol Spectrum Disorders and Attention-Deficit/Hyperactivity Disorder – A meta-analysis, *The Journal of Child Psychology and Psychiatry, 57(2)*, 116-131.

Klassen, R. M., & Chiu, M. M. (2010). Effects on teachers' self-efficacy and job satisfaction: Teacher gender, years of experience, and job stress. *Journal of Educational Psychology, 102*, 741–756. doi:10.1037/a0019237

Klassen, R. M., & Chiu, M. M. (2011). The occupational commitment and intention to quit of practicing and preservice teachers: Influence of self-efficacy, job stress, and teaching context. *Contemporary Educational Psychology, 36,* 114–129. doi:10.1016/j.cedpsych.2011.01.002

Mahoney, J. L., Durklan, J. A. & Weissberg, R. P. (2018). An update on social and emotional learning outcome research. *Kappan.* https://kappanonline.org/social-emotional-learning-outcome-research-mahoney-durlak-weissberg/

McCarthy, C. J., Lambert, R. C., O'Donnell, M., & Melendres, L. T. (2009). The relation of elementary teachers' experience, stress, and coping resources to burnout symptoms. *Elementary School Journal, 109,* 282–300. doi:10.1086/592308

Miller, C. (2023). Anxious stomach aches and headaches. *Child Mind Institute.* https://childmind.org/article/anxious-stomach-aches-and-headaches/

Mitten, H.R. (2013), Evidence-based practice guidelines for Fetal Alcohol Spectrum Disorder and literacy and learning, *International Journal of Special Education 28(3),* 44-57

Office on Child Abuse and Neglect, Children's Bureau. (2018). *Child protection in families experiencing domestic violence.* Child Welfare. https://www.childwelfare.gov/pubPDFs/domesticviolence2018.pdf.

Paley, B. and O'Connor, M.J., (2011). Behavioral interventions for children and adolescents with Fetal Alcohol Spectrum Disorders. *Alcohol Research and Health, 34(1),* 64-75.

Purvis, K., Cross, D. R., & Sunshine, W. L. (2007). *The connected child: Bring hope and healing to your adoptive family.* McGraw-Hill.

Reyes-Portillo, J., Elias, M., Parker, S. & Rosenblatt, J. (2013). Promoting educational equity in disadvantaged youth: The role of resilience and social-emotional learning. In S. Goldstein & R. Brooks (Eds), *Handbook of resilience in children.* Springer.

Ryan, R. M. & Deci, E. L. (2017). *Self-determination theory: Basic psychological needs in motivation, development, and wellness.* Guilford Press.

Schonert-Reichl, K. A. (2017). Social and emotional learning and teachers. *The Future of Children, 27*(1), 137–155. http://www.jstor.org/stable/44219025

Schultz, Q. (2022). *Servant teaching—Practices for renewing Christian higher education.* Edenridge Press, LLC.

Shotsberger, P. & Freytag, C. (Eds.). (2020). *How shall we then care? A Christian educator's guide to caring for self, learners, colleagues, and community.* Wipf and Stock.

Wallace Foundation (2021). *Find out how to build social and emotional learning skills.* https://www.wallacefoundation.org/promos2/pages/navigating-social-and-emotional-learning.aspx?utm_id=go_cmp-827908937_adg-45169333809_ad-509434887038_kwd-375026528837_dev-c_ext-_prd-_mca-_sig-Cj0KCQjwtO-kBhDIARIsAL6LoreCvaItBEvoKuYE7kQK5lrO2j3QghyZind5T5hxFwD6JwOPFM710nIaAtpfEALw_wcB&utm_source=google&gclid=Cj0KCQjwtO-kBhDIARIsAL6LoreCvaItBEvoKuYE7kQK5lrO2j3QghyZind5T5hxFwD6JwOPFM710nIaAtpfEALw_wcB

Wildenhaus, C. (2019). *Helping children manage anxiety at school.* Self-published.

About the Editors and Contributors

Valerie Flanagan (PhD, University of the Cumberlands) is the graduate chair in CU's School of Education. She previously served as a middle school science and STEM educator. She has been a middle school teacher of the year recipient, and currently facilitates courses in graduate teacher leadership and school improvement programs. Valerie's areas of research interest include social emotional learning and trauma-informed teaching.

Robin Magruder (Ed.D., University of Kentucky) is the undergraduate chair for the CU School of Education, and teaches undergraduate and graduate courses as well. Before joining the faculty at Campbellsville University, she was an elementary and middle school math teacher for twelve years. Robin has won numerous awards, and was the university's distinguished tenure professor in 2018. Her areas of research interest are in elementary pedagogy and mathematics education. Robin is the mother of three adult children.

Rocky Wallace (DSL, Regent University) teaches graduate education leadership courses for CU, and has helped develop similar programs at Asbury University and Morehead State University. He is a former teacher and coach, former principal of a U.S. Blue Ribbon School, served in the Highly Skilled Educator Program at the Kentucky Department of Education, and served as director of instructional support and adult education at KEDC (education co-op in Ashland, KY). This is his twelfth book project with Rowman & Littlefield.

* * *

Kerri Adkins (Ed.D., Western Kentucky University) currently teaches education courses at CU. Before transitioning to higher education, she devoted her time to educating high school students in the areas of chemistry, biology, environmental science, and physical science. She resides in central Kentucky with her husband and two youngest sons.

Jane Bragg (Ed.D., Liberty University) has been a special education teacher her entire career. When serving in K-12, she taught in the MSD self-contained classroom—both elementary and high school, throughout her career. She earned her doctorate degree in curriculum and instruction (special education), and currently teaches special education classes at CU.

Lisa Fulks (PhD, University of Louisville) is the option six coordinator in the CU School of Education. Her areas of research interest are in special education and social emotional learning. She was a teacher and administrator for over thirty years with Jefferson County Public Schools in Louisville, Kentucky.

Holly Kay Graham (Ed.D., Carson Newman University) teaches students earning their master's degrees in teaching at CU. After college, she spent seven years in Russia as a sports missionary, working with underprivileged children and teenagers. Later, she taught middle school students reading and English in the Appalachia mountains of Tennessee.

Kalem Grasham (Ed.D., University of the Cumberlands) is entering his twenty-fifth year in public education. Kalem has served as a special education and regular education teacher, assistant principal, principal, and in his current role as director of federal programs for Garrard County Schools. He is an adjunct professor in CU's graduate education leadership program.

Marilyn Goodwin (PhD, Capella University) is a professor of education at Campbellsville University. Marilyn began teaching in the Early Childhood Education program at CU in 2010. She has a master of divinity in Christian education from the Southern Baptist Theological Seminary. She is married to Rev. Michael Goodwin and they have one son, Micah Goodwin.

Charles "Chuck" Hamilton (Ed.D., University of Kentucky) is a former math teacher, coach, assistant principal, principal, and school superintendent. He is highly regarded across Kentucky for his experience in school leadership, and previously led CU's pre-service teacher prep program. He currently teaches graduate education leadership courses for CU.

Ellen Hamilton-Ford (Ed.D, Spalding University) has been an educator for more than thirty years and currently teaches at CU. Her background includes teaching early elementary grades, and instructional leadership as an assistant principal. She focuses on teaching early learning skills with an emphasis on positive socialemotional learning.

Laura Beth Hayes (Ed.D., Western Kentucky University) has had an accomplished career as a teacher, assistant principal, and principal, with three degrees from CU. She writes and provides presentations on SEL and trauma-informed care, and was the keynote speaker at CU's Excellence in Teaching Awards, 2019, and graduate school commencement, 2021.

Jeffrey D. Herron (Ed.D., Eastern Kentucky University) is an associate professor and diversity and inclusion coordinator with the School of Education at CU. A published author, Jeffrey's research interests include family and community partnerships, mental health, child development, cultural diversity, African American families, non-residential fathers, juvenile delinquency, and poverty.

Deborah Holt (MA, Campbellsville University) has been in the education field for over forty years. She has taught all ages, from infants to adult learners in higher education and military students in advanced individual training. She has a master's degree in interdisciplinary early childhood education and is currently working on her doctoral degree in curriculum and instruction at Oakland City University.

Joetta Kelly (Ed.D., Western Kentucky University) teaches in the CU Master's of School Counseling Program. She is also a counselor, previously served in church ministry, taught art and physical education, and has written and illustrated several children's books. She lives in Murray, Kentucky and enjoys her three children, their spouses, and her five grand-girls.

Elisha Lawrence (Ed.D., Eastern Kentucky University) is the assessment coordinator in CU's School of Education. She also teaches various undergraduate educator preparation courses related to the field of literacy, and graduate courses in ESL and school counseling. Her doctoral concentration was in educational land policy studies.

Kathryn E. H. Smith (Ed.D., University of Kentucky) teaches literacy courses at CU. She enjoys reading research literature related to culture, the Appalachian region, and reading comprehension. Her favorite text to read and study is the Bible. Her doctoral concentration was in instruction and administration, with an emphasis in literacy.

Franklin B. Thomas (Ed.D., Eastern Kentucky University) teaches graduate education leadership courses and is the assistant chair of CU's School of Education graduate program. He has served in the Kentucky Department of Education's Highly Skilled Educator cohort, and as an assistant principal, principal, and in several district-level executive leadership positions.

Jeff Wiesman (Ed.D., Aurora University) mentors and teaches pre-service educators. Prior to coming to CU, he taught at Houghton University for eight years. Previously, he spent twenty years teaching middle and high school mathematics. His doctoral focus was curriculum and instruction. He enjoys kayaking, hiking, and traveling to new places with his family.